The FRESH Classroom:

Why Culturally Relevant Education Can't Wait!

Stephanie Boyce, Ph.D.

The FRESH Classroom: Why Culturally Relevant Education Can't Wait!

© 2021 by Stephanie Boyce, Ph.D.
www.stephanieboyce.com

Published by Stephanie Boyce & Associates, LLC, Dallas, Texas

Library of Congress Control Number:: 2021920544

Paperback ISBN: 978-0-578-30585-1

Ebook ISBN: 978-0-578-30586-8

Audiobook ISBN: 978-0-578-30587-5

Dedication

To my fearless daughter, Amari Boyce. Always remember your daily affirmations:

I am strong.
I am smart.
I am fearfully and wonderfully made in the image of God.
I can move mountains.
I can do ANYTHING!
Amen.

This book is my offering to a world that needs love like never before.
I pray you'll be a reflection of that love.
Mungu akubariki

Contents

Part III: Data Don't Lie

Introduction

"It is necessary to align our professed values with our real actions."
~ Robin Diangelo

In the past, I carefully navigated educational spaces mincing words in my best efforts to ensure the respectability, palatability, and acceptability of my words. That time is gone. Now, I stand with a bullhorn on the steps of the school buildings of America. I am ushering out an era when people of color engaged, inauthentically, in professional spaces to avoid labels like "race-baiter" and being accused of playing the "race card" when engaging people in the disconcerting conversations about the realities of racial injustice in schools and society at large. I am admonishing everyone from educational leaders to tax-paying citizens to wake up to what decades of research in schools have shown us to be necessary for all classrooms, especially those serving students of color. At this moment, I stand flat-footed, shouting to anyone who will read these words: CULTURALLY RELEVANT EDUCATION CANNOT WAIT!

Perhaps this sentiment may sound familiar to those who study history and remember Dr. Martin Luther King, Jr., writing to his fellow clergymen in his famed *Letter from a Birmingham Jail*. Although he wrote those words in 1963, the sense of urgency he proclaimed from that jail cell resounds in this current 21st century moment. That echoing urgency is the reason I have employed those words as the subtitle for this book. The fact that, decades later, the vicious jaws of racial injustice are still trapping us is the reason that we educators CANNOT WAIT. The fact that 2020 found us in the middle of an "eruption of consciousness" due to the lynching of another unarmed Black man, George Floyd, in the streets of Minneapolis is the reason we educators CANNOT WAIT. The fact that demonstrations spilled into the streets, while privileged bystanders "deplore[d] the demonstrations taking place... [when] the city's White power structure left the Negro community with no alternative" (King, 1963) is the reason we educators CANNOT WAIT. The fact that well-documented opportunity gaps continue to be the reality for millions of students of color, decades after 1954's *Brown v. Board of Education*, is the reason we educators CANNOT WAIT. The fact that disciplinary data "clearly shows that students of color are less safe, more restrained, and pushed out of school more than other students" (Balingit, 2008) is the reason we educators CANNOT WAIT.

The time for passively suggesting best practices as an option has come to an end. It is time for educators to courageously depart from traditional classroom practices that have, despite the good intentions of many, colonized classrooms and further marginalized students of color for too long. This is the moment for decisive movement toward amplifying student voices and better understanding the cultural capital of the communities from which they emerge. If we are the caring and empathetic professionals we profess to be in our philosophies of education, we have to focus our critique and analysis on ourselves and commit to something new. There is no better time than now, and no one is as optimistic and hopeful about what all our classrooms can provide for students as I am.

As you begin your journey to cultivating more culturally responsive classrooms, campuses, and society, my prayer is that you read these pages with an open heart and mind. When you feel yourself having a strong reaction to something I've written, pause to reflect or even make a written note of what just triggered you and why. Challenge yourself to keep reading through your moments of discomfort and know that this reflection will empower you to gain some knowledge that will help your pedagogy, students, classroom, and campus. You will become FRESHer for the students you serve by the end. This awareness and reflection is part of the work to which we must commit ourselves if we are to transform into culturally relevant educators. Let's do it!

PART I

Get Ya' Mind Right

Math Deficits 101

(Because Blinded Teachers Don't See Deficits)

"Every child deserves a champion—an adult who will never give up on them, who understands the power of connection, and insists that they become the best that they can possibly be."
~ Rita Pierson

No kid wakes up and says, "I want to suck today! I can't wait to go to school and fail!" I assume the same to be true about teachers. However, Mr. D was different. At first sight, his square shoulders and box hair cut gave off the impression he may have been a military man in his former life. He stood at the front of the classroom, writing at the board, as we all sat stalely in single-filed rows with all eyes on him. Mr. D was a lecturing kind of teacher, and I was a 9th-grade girl. A student liked by my peers, a cheerleader, who had decided to enroll herself in pre-AP biology, pre-AP geography, and pre-AP English, but I had severe math deficits.

In 9th grade, I had to take Algebra I. For the life of me, I could not understand why the hell someone found it necessary to terrorize students with the idea of mixing numbers with letters and calling it algebra. I mean, letters were for English class. Man, I loved letters and English class! I had a way with words. I was a writer and an avid reader. But numbers were always for math class, and they always rendered me useless in any situation.

For this reason, Mr. D didn't get the well-behaved, critical thinking, interactive, and cooperative Stephanie seen by other teachers in their classes most days. Mr.

D was unfortunate enough to meet the I-don't-give-a-damn alter ego of my 9th-grade self. I call her Steph B.

Steph B was the student with a chip perfectly balanced on her shoulder anytime she entered the classroom from the hallway. Many educators reading this have had a Steph B in their classrooms. However, for the teacher untrained in recognizing red flags that may indicate a student has seriously embarrassing deficits, a student like Steph B can easily be labeled a "bad kid" or "a persistent classroom disruption" and written off accordingly. Mr. D was one of those teachers, and I was his worst nightmare, a quick-witted class clown who could hijack instructional time at the drop of a dime. I was a ticking time bomb.

This is the most toxic kind of student to deal with because they use their power and leverage it against the teacher. When Mr. D inquired about my homework, I retorted with a smart-ass reply. When he called on me to answer questions aloud (while he knew I could not answer), I voiced my lack of concern or made deflecting comments that got a laugh out of the class. When he turned his back to us to write on the board, I may or may not have done things like thrown a paper ball or yelled out obscenities. I was a complete terror to Mr. D, and he was the worst type of teacher to have encountered a student like me. He was blind. Not literally, but professionally blind. He was so enamored with the "what" (my terrible behavior and antics) that he never took time to analyze the "why" (the root cause of my behavior).

To this day, I believe one diagnostic assessment or parent-teacher conference, forcing us to look at the why behind the what of my behavior, could have been the difference between me overcoming my fear of math and adding another name to the list of teachers who changed my life over the years. On the contrary, Mr. D is the teacher at the top of the list of those I have tried and convicted of the most heinous crime known in teaching: Educational Malpractice.

Instead of trying to get past the layers of disrespect that adorned my persona when I entered his classroom, Mr. D took the easy road out as some educators do. He made one of the biggest mistakes an educator could make: He took my disrespect personally. It was a strike to his ego and for all the class to see. I had to be handled, neutralized, annihilated. He had to make an example out of me.

So, what did he do? After writing me a constant stream of referrals and realizing they were not going to switch me to another class, he finally made a deal with the Assistant Principal (AP). If the AP let me report to the front office during his class period, he would send the math work for me to complete independently. In exchange for me and my smart mouth not coming to his class, he gave me 70 each of the grading periods that followed. I was his sacrificial lamb. My Mom would see the report card and note that I was passing, so she had no concern. Meanwhile, the deficits I experienced that year had lasting implications for the remaining years of math to come in high school, college, and even in my Ph.D. program (doctoral-level stats are from the math devil).

Coming back to teach at that same high school, years later, with the same student demographics (low income, majority-minoritized students), I always knew one thing to be fact: If a kid has to choose between being seen as a dummy or a smart ass in front of their peers, the Steph B's you encounter will always opt for the latter. When I encountered a student who attempted to use bad behavior to escape the reading and writing we did in English class, it was a red flag for me. It was a Steph B with a tough persona and a deep desire to cover up the truth about being a smart kid who was struggling.

The question then becomes, "What will you do?" Whoa to the teacher who takes a student's behavior personally. This teacher will overreact and be blinded by the what and never get to the why. The teacher who wears specs with professional 20/20 will see a child's backlash for what it really is: A cry for help—a defense mechanism. Don't get me wrong, students like Steph B definitely deserve consequences for their disrespectful behaviors. The next question then becomes, "What else?" How do you work to get to the why behind that student's what? Those are the defining moments for teachers and students. The effort to get to the why empowers the courageous conversations and conferences that have the power to change the trajectory of students' lives forever.

Chapter 1

Get Ya' Mind Right

"In a growth mindset, challenges are exciting rather than threatening. So rather than thinking, oh, I'm going to reveal my weaknesses, you say, wow, here's a chance to grow."
~ Carol S. Dweck, Ph.D.

My name is Dr. Stephanie Boyce. I am an educator, a multi-passionate entrepreneur, and an advocate for kids. I have a Master's degree and Ph.D. in education. I've been a principal, assistant principal, instructional coach, and most importantly, a teacher. A high school English Language Arts Reading (ELAR) teacher, to be exact (shout out ELAR teachers). Since I am a professional and the author of this book, these credentials matter, so when I train teachers in my FRESH Workshops, I always lead with those facts. However, I also find it equally important to mention that I was Steph B before I was any of those things.

I ask teachers to imagine the one student they wish they could send away to alternative school or trade to another teacher's class indefinitely, and then I explain to them how I was THAT kid for some of my teachers. In middle school, I did two placements in alternative school; I was arrested at 16, ran away from home, fought my peers, fought my Mom, and made defiance a way of life. But despite how many bad choices I made, I was never a bad kid. I still cringe and challenge any adult who labels a kid "bad" to this day because I *was* that kid.

The truth of my experience is this: Kids sometimes have unhealthy ways of expressing and dealing with the pain and fear they experience daily. That's why I'm constantly challenging educators to get to the why behind a kid's behavior and don't get stuck at the what (I know I've discussed this already), so let's look at some examples:

What: A kid fights at school often.
Possible Why: The kid feels the need to ensure respect amongst his/her peers.

What: A kid regularly disrupts the lesson during instructional time.
Possible Why: The kid has learning deficits that manifest in misbehavior to avoid embarrassment.

What: A kid is compulsively tardy to school in the mornings.
Possible Why: Kid works a job until late at night during the school week.

Please don't misunderstand; students do need consequences when they make bad choices. I'm reinforcing here the need for us to do a better job working to understand why, especially regarding historically marginalized student demographics (Black, Latinx, and resource-limited students), and working toward addressing those more profound issues. In many cases, cultural clashes between students and teachers are at the root of many of the disciplinary disparities we witness in schools.

For example, I often share the multiple situations I had while working in urban-characteristic schools with young men who chose to wear their pants below their waist or "sagging." Since I was from the area where my students lived and often saw my own younger brothers in the faces of the young men I served, I understood the importance of respect as a form of cultural capital in these types of disciplinary exchanges. So, when I saw a student like (let's call him Devante) coming down the hallway while I was on hall duty, I could yell from across the hallway, "Devante, pull those pants up NOW!" and hope he would consent without incident. No behavioral escalation, no problem, on to the next task. However, more often than not, this approach would result in Devante shooting back a smart-mouthed retort in response to being called out. That would have led me to write him a discipline referral to show him who was in control. There he would have punitive consequences for the disrespect I had endured while simply trying to enforce the dress code policy.

However, the second option to rectifying this situation is more effective. Time after time, instead of berating Devante loudly from across the hallway (something he may have perceived as disrespectful to him), I would get into close proximity to Devante while leading in with a light-hearted welcome like "Good morning, sir! Happy Monday," then directing him to comply with the dress code rule, while inserting a little humor by telling him, "Devante, can you get those pants up for me, so I don't have to see your red underwear this morning? Thank you, sir, make it a great Monday!"

While some educators may hear such an exchange and think it's too much, I've had countless incidents like the one mentioned above that never once escalated to disciplinary action or created a hallway standoff between a kid and me. The truth is students appreciate respect, as much as adults do, so my policy was to talk to them the way I would speak to a colleague if I needed to communicate the same message to them. It's not deep; it's just respect.

Decide Who You'll Be

Nobody can write a book that tells you the best way to connect to your students. To gain insights into your students, you have to communicate with them. Become a student of your students. What are they into? What's going on in the hallways? What music is flooding their earbuds? What niche hobbies are they rushing home to? No one can tell you what students need but the students you serve even though educators spend millions of dollars in a constant search for the next book, gadget, and app to help them become more effective with their craft. I have discovered that no professional development, summer retreat, or wittily-titled book can transform a teacher's craft, if they are not open to building meaningful relationships with kids. Point blank. Period.

On the contrary, a fully invested teacher with a heart to connect and cultivate authentic relationships with students can add tools to their toolkit that make magic happen in the classroom. So, before you get into all that is the FRESH classroom, ask yourself: "Which teacher am I?" Not on the surface level, but in your heart. How much time have you spent talking to kids about things other than the grade you assigned and the content you teach? Do you spend time in their community at all? Reflect honestly and know that your willingness to connect in deep and meaningful ways with students will be the difference between you getting your classroom FRESH or not.

Let the Cynicism Go

It pains me to see a culture amongst teachers where cynicism has become rewarded and almost celebrated in the profession. The rise of negative hashtags, memes, and even comedians gaining popularity fueled by educators' complaining culture is all the rage. I wouldn't dare act as though I've never had my cynical moments over the years doing the hard work on campuses. Still, I believe there is a stark difference between having moments of negative feelings, thoughts, and cynical retorts and embracing a movement that wears self-deprecation like a badge of honor.

The problem is that the same people who give time, energy, and momentum to negative teacher talk:

1. Lead classes full of students who should be getting inspired and uplifted,
2. Want to demand the people outside the profession take them seriously, pay them their worth, and respect them as the professionals who make all other professions possible.

I want to start this book by making a bold statement: If We Want People to Take Educators Seriously, We Must First Take Ourselves Seriously.

From our daily attire choices to how we talk about the profession. I can't tell you how many times I've had to stop myself from going in on a Facebook post or an Instagram comment in response to a teacher claiming how trifling parents are in their school or how students never take ownership of their learning. I'm not saying I've never felt frustration when parents don't answer my calls or when students refuse to do the work. What I'm saying is some teachers use those (and other extenuating circumstances) to justify the opportunity gaps students encounter in their schools and classrooms.

Don't close the book yet.

Stay with me for a minute.

One of my favorite educators, Ron Clark, of the Ron Clark Academy in Atlanta, Georgia, admonishes us to make education "Young, Fun, Sexy, and Hot." It sounds like a bit much, but at its core, the message is simple, WE as educators bring the good vibes and magic to the profession.

Do we need to be engaged in combating faulty legislation that isn't good for schools? *Yes.*

Should we voice our concerns as professionals? *Sure.*

But a constant barrage of negative self-talk only depreciates the power of the profession. We shouldn't talk that way to ourselves. We are the heartbeats of schools. We bring the party and keep it going! Without us, schools don't pop, sparkle, or shine. We have to believe we are, in fact, *the shit*. Then act like it!

Own Your Successes (and Failures)

In 2012, I taught 9th Grade English Language Arts when Texas rolled out its newest, shiniest, most challenging tests, the State of Texas Assessments of Academic Readiness, better known as the STAAR test. By this time, we had mastered preparing our students for the Texas Assessment of Knowledge and Skills (TAKS) test, and I was accustomed to about 90% or more of my students passing this test the first time around. I owned it. When they did well, I strutted around, all full of hubris, feeling like all my hard work was rewarded vicariously through their success on one assessment. So, what happened the first year they took the STAAR test? You guessed it. They bombed.

I believe about 50% of my students passed that first administration of the STAAR test in 2012. What did I do? Blame the state for making a terrible test? Blame parents for not coming to parent-teacher conferences and working harder with students at home? Blame students for not coming to additional tutorial times to prep for the test? Blame administration for not better preparing me how to strategize more precisely with my lessons? No. I marched right to my principal's office and told her I quit! I told her I wasn't equipped to prepare these kids for success in these new evolving circumstances, and I would rather her hire someone who could.

Of course, she laughed at what she considered my theatrics and encouraged me to take the weekend to rest and step away from the numbers and come back Monday. While my response may have been a little extra (I am who I am), one thing is true: I owned it. I didn't look around at all the broken parts of the system to point fingers and shift blame. If these students come to THIS classroom to learn from THIS teacher and I am a trained and certified professional, THIS outcome hinges on THIS teacher. It's tough for some teachers to do, but we have to get past the blame-shifting and step up to the plate. We have to be willing to own the truth that teachers are the #1 difference makers for students mastering the curriculum.

Even when they come into classrooms several years below grade level, teachers can lift them. I say this with all confidence because of what I've observed in my classrooms and others. The educator's ability to shift from a helpless victim to a bad-ass is a real phenomenon, but it's also a choice. So again, I ask you to reflect and ask yourself, "Where do I stand?" Will you be a helpless, lowly teacher at the bottom of the totem pole, at the mercy of administrators, and abandoned by absent parents? Or will you be a FRESH teacher who maximizes classroom minutes, makes learning in your classroom an experience, and leverages the school community's resources in ways that leave a legacy in schools. The truth is, either way, you'll get a paycheck, but only one is a game-changer for kids. If you chose the latter, this book is an excellent tool for you. Now let's get FRESH!

Jan & James Reject

(Because Race and Culture Are Not The Same)

"Elitism is the slur directed at merit by mediocrity."
~ Sydney J. Harris

In my junior year of high school, I found myself in a suburban, diversely populated (but primarily White) high school. It was then that I first encountered REAL bougie Black people. Many folks will tell you that bougie Blacks are much more pretentious than wealthy White people. I came to learn the truth behind that belief my junior year of high school. That school year, I had become acquainted with a senior girl whom I will call Katy. Around Christmas time, Katy invited me to the annual Christmas party for an elite organization of African Americans her family belonged to; I'll call it Jan & James. I was super excited to join her (after all, she was the definition of affluence, and I was one of the "apartment kids").

I pulled up to the estates' entry where she lived and immediately felt out of my league, but you know I'm always up for a challenge if you know me. I sat up a little straighter and attempted to be the best bougie version of myself. LOL.

The house was a mini mansion by my standards. I found out, that day, she had lawyer parents. Now, it all made sense. These folks were clearly out of my league. I had opted to wear an all-black, one-piece jumpsuit (for shame). Meanwhile, the other girls were in cocktail dresses. Nevertheless, we got to the party (in the ballroom of a downtown hotel), and I had the time of my life. The atmosphere was great, the people were welcoming, and I was totally enjoying all the young men dressed like distinguished gentlemen (pants pulled up, no tats, or gold teeth). I mean, this was different. LOL. This party was the type of social scene I didn't know existed before that night.

I quickly learned this world of Black excellence had intended to be invisible from kids like me. After our night of dancing and fun, I went to Katy to thank her for the invite to the party and express my interest in joining the Jan & James organization. She quickly extinguished my excitement by informing me that it was not possible. The only way to gain membership was for one of the mothers to invite my mother. I mean, clearly, I had a mother, but the tone of her response was clear. I didn't have the type of mother they would have in this social circle. I had, on the contrary, gained limited access to breathe in the air up there, but I was not in any way to get too comfortable. After all, I did stay in the apartments down the street and not in a mini-mansion. I knew exactly what she meant in that moment.

All these years later, I still feel the sting of rejection when anyone mentions that organization to me. Hissssss! (Hissing is a sound I literally make out loud to express my disdain when necessary). Now that I'm older, I have loved ones that are members of that organization. I see the remarkable social gatherings and programs they put on for their kids, and it really seems great. Nonetheless, somewhere inside me sits the sting of that rejection that still leaves me feeling like Steph B, a girl from the hood who believed in the myth of meritocracy even though money and status mattered more.

Chapter 2

Race vs. Culture

"A fundamental problem facing us is the way in which systems of domination and exploitation persist and reproduce themselves without being consciously recognized by the people involved."
~ Michael W. Apple, *Education and Power*

Let's address the elephant in the classroom. Many educators work on campuses where they are racially or culturally different from most students they serve. This is not breaking news. However, by starting conversations in The FRESH Classroom Workshops, many teachers can define the difference between race and culture, although they may use the terms interchangeably in conversation. So, here's your first pop quiz. What's the difference? Pause and write your definitions below (don't cheat, I can see you!)

Race

_____

_____

_____

Culture

_____

_____

_____

I can remember the first time I had to think deeply about the difference between race and culture. I was sitting in a workshop with Dr. Kimberly McLeod when she handed me a blank index card and asked us to define the two terms. It was difficult for me to differentiate at first, but for the sake of social science and our professional conversations, we must do this task.

Now, I start each of my FRESH Workshops with that same challenge. The answer I give participants, as you can find many ways to define these two words in the research, comes from Tara Yosso (2005). She defines race as a "biological concept that refers to the gene frequencies in a population. Races are differentiated by inherited characteristics, and racial categories are often defined based on physical appearance." On the contrary, she defines culture as the "behaviors and values that are learned, shared, and exhibited by a group of people."

I've encountered people in workshops that insist that race is a nonfactor and there is only one race: The Human Race. And while that may be true on a molecular level (I'm no scientist), we refer to race as a social construct in our conversations. While you may peel back your skin and not identify race and we all bleed red and originate from one sole creator, race has long been used as a social construct to define, divide, and disenfranchise people worldwide. That's just a historical fact.

I still encounter people who shut down at the mere mention of race, racism, social justice, Black Lives Matter, or anything else they believe will usher in a conversation they deem political in nature. Honestly, nothing should be less political than a conversation about race because racism is as American as America herself. Ignoring the fact that these United States' wealth was built by 400 years of free labor by enslaved Africans is just intellectually dishonest. To move forward with honest conversations around race and culture and their impact on our daily decisions and practices (both conscious and unconscious), we have to start with the hard truth that people of color, and Black folks especially, have endured state-sanctioned violence, disrespect, degradation, and second-class citizenry since the birth of this nation. Read that again.

Centuries later, we see the impact of the sinful stain of slavery and the racial subjugation on people of color in our country when we examine the numbers on an institutional basis. We see, with unabashed consistency, White people sit in seats of institutional power and control politically and economically across the board:

- Twenty wealthiest Americans: 100% White
- US Congress: 77% White
- US Governors: 94% White
- Philanthropic foundation CEOs: 92% White
- Philanthropic foundation Boards: 89% White
- Management of Financial Services: 81% White
- Venture Capitalist: 86% White
- Angel Investors: 96% White
- Educational Administrators: 68% White
- Teachers: 79% White
- Full-time college professors: 90% White
- People who control book publishing: 76% White

While none of us currently living are responsible for creating the racial disparities baked into every institution across America, we have the power to disrupt and dismantle the status quo or to help maintain and preserve it. In her bestselling 2020 book *Caste*, Isabel Wilkerson masterfully illustrates the idea of the American caste system as an old, dilapidated house that we've all inherited (think home renovation show). None of us alive today is responsible for the house's current condition, but it is still in need of a total gut job. An overhaul. A reckoning. We have to find our way forward together because we will all occupy the house together.

Communities of Color

Because race was used as a tool to divide us for so long, we see still see overlap in the cultural experiences of people with similar racial backgrounds and geographical locations. It's the reason we see trending hashtags like #BlackThanksgiving, #LatinoAmerica, and others that resonate with so many people from many different geographical areas. It's the reason why I can travel to schools in hoods from Oak Cliff, Texas, to the South Side of Chicago, and feel perfectly comfortable and not clutch my handbag when I walk past a Black man in sagging pants. I don't see a threat; I see my brother in his eyes. It's the same sentiment expressed by Beyoncé and Jay Z, in the hit song "Black Effect", when they say, "I'm good on any MLK Boulevard." We appreciate the concepts of inter-hood appreciation and respect for the role communities of color play in incubating the success of many people whose greatness started within their zip codes. The spirit, hope, and hustle of the people who bustle up and down the streets in the hood is evident. We share knowledge of the unspoken truths and realities that govern the hood. I could go on, but I'll pause for now.

The truth is that for the richness I see in the hood, another person can look and see every negative aspect of these same communities. Many people can't see the heart, soul, and beauty of the people because they view the environment from a deficit purview. I won't pretend that there are no negative aspects of the hood or that I don't empathize with the despair of the economic drought and exploitation felt by many people in under-resourced neighborhoods. Still, people who look upon these communities with pity and disgrace are not necessarily allies in the fight for social justice.

Cultural Nuance

I may share racial characteristics with another Black person, but many cultural differences shape the reality of who we are and what we value. These are nuances that suggest merely having a teacher of color in a classroom with students of color doesn't immediately mean the teacher can make a cultural connection or have an understanding of what their students deal with every day. I can recall observing many White teachers over the years who built relationships, leaned into their students' interests and lived experiences, and managed to have great success with students of color.

Take a second to reflect on the question of differences between people within the same cultural groups, then write as many answers as possible in the space that follows. What are some cultural differences that exist within racial groups? I'll give you one, as an example, religious differences. For example, I may have a sibling of the same race and bloodline, but we may discover that we have some vastly different values, beliefs, and behaviors because I am a Christian and align my lifestyle according to biblical principles. They may live a lifestyle based on a separate set of principles and values. That's just one example. Think of some other cultural differences that exist within racial groups. Write as many as you can here:

⌐ Cultural Differences Within Racial Groups ⌐

_____

_____

_____

_____

_____

Please don't skip making this list! Go back. LOL. No seriously, in The FRESH Classroom's Workshops, we have to pause to discuss these. Often, educators don't take time to fully understand the class, gender, generational, and geographical differences. These are some of the differences that often fuel the cultural clashes that exist in classrooms every day. Think about it. I've spent my fair share of time in the hood. *Side note: I wouldn't say I like to sugarcoat terms like "the hood" because I don't ascribe negative connotations to the term. I love everything about the hood, from the fried fish baskets, barber/beauty salons, lively churches, and the people's authenticity. * For this reason, I've always taught in the hood and had success in the schools that I was blessed to serve. While my paycheck changed my economic status, it never changed my belief that many people in the hood are misunderstood and underappreciated by many of those employed to provide services to their communities (i.e., educators, law enforcement officers, healthcare providers, etc.). I'll explore that misunderstanding more deeply in my next book.

For this reason, I never wanted to work anywhere else. I believe in the students in those schools and communities; hell, I was the students in those schools. On the contrary, I spent my fair share of time skeptical of educator prep programs that assign teachers to the hood for a specified term. That is because I know that people who don't have a heart for the hood should not be teaching there. I don't mean to suggest that educators cannot build their cultural competence to serve students of varying cultures better; it's just been my experience that far too many educators expect the opposite to happen when they inhabit educational spaces. In his 2016 book, *For White Folks Who Teach in the Hood... and the Rest of Y'all Too*, one of the dopest scholars I know, Dr. Chris Emdin, puts it this way:

> In schools, urban youth are expected to leave their day-to-day experiences and emotions at the door and assimilate into the culture of schools. This process of personal repression is in itself traumatic and directly impacts what happens in the classroom.... Failure to prepare teachers to appreciate the psychic spaces students occupy inevitably limits their effectiveness. Some teachers understand that students come from places beyond the classroom and can acknowledge that these places have an effect on students and the spaces they occupy. However, many teachers cannot see beyond their immediate location (the school) and therefore have a very limited understanding of space. Many more are taught to ignore psychic space altogether, and therefore cannot fathom what it must be like for students to whom the classroom is a breeding ground for traumatic experiences.

This book and his latest, "Ratchedemic" are absolute must-reads, as Emdin spends a lot more time diving into his research on reality pedagogy and leveraging hip-hop education in classrooms that foster the authenticity of students and teachers.

Levels of Culture

In an effort to display an understanding and awareness of their students' cultural composition, some teachers get stuck on the surface, such as creating intricate handshakes, playing popular songs, or dressing in particular ways to better relate to students. While these efforts are steps in becoming more culturally connected to their students, they reflect what Zaretta Hammond calls the surface culture.

In her 2015 book, *Culturally Responsive Teaching and The Brain*, Hammond explains the three levels of culture as follows:

1. Surface Culture
2. Shallow Culture
3. Deep Culture

First, Hammond explains surface culture as being the "observable and concrete elements of culture such as food, dress, music, and holidays." These concrete aspects, or cultural displays, are easier to identify and replicate when desired, but they are not indicators of more significant cultural elements.

The second level, shallow culture, however, speaks to the unstated rules "around everyday social interactions and norms, such as courtesy, attitudes toward elders, nature of friendships, concepts of time, personal space between people, nonverbal communication, rules about eye contact, or appropriate touching." I find this distinction to be of utmost importance in schools as teachers and students frequently find themselves in the throes of cultural clashes that result at this shallow level. For instance, I grew up understanding that looking a person in the eyes during a conversation was a non-negotiable element of respect. Even as I write this, I can only imagine my mother or father speaking to me as I glance off in the distance or down at the ground. Consider my surprise when I learned that making eye contact with an authority figure was considered disrespectful to people in other cultural groups. I was dumbfounded. Now in hindsight, it makes perfect sense. Eye contact, a non-verbal form of communication, can show aggression or strength, express attraction and desire, or demonstrate complete disdain.

The interpretation is entirely up to each individual's cultural inclinations and perceptions.

Lastly, deep culture refers to the "unconscious assumptions that govern our worldview. It also contains the cosmology (view of good or bad) that guides ethics, spirituality, health, and theories of group harmony (i.e., competition or cooperation)." I think the best, and sadly ever-relevant, example here is how people respond to police shootings of unarmed Black people in America. One group of people will say the officer's use of force was utterly unnecessary and indicative of our criminal justice system's blatant disregard of Black lives. At the same time, another group of people will insist that a Black person with the audacity to resist an assault on their bodies by an officer of the law is deserving of whatever action the officer deems necessary to gain control of the situation. Further still, each group of people will be able to find a cable news station, newspaper source, or Facebook group that agrees with and further confirms their view about this issue.

Another example can be seen in award-winning journalist and news anchor Tashara Parker's "Rooted" series, which aired in 2021. This series of interviews unpacked the stories of Black people and their lived experiences with natural hair discrimination in schools and the workplace. Those unfamiliar with Black culture and the deep-rooted social and emotional trauma historically associated with Black hair and the American experience were shocked to discover the many layers to this issue. This deeper awareness gives people the context necessary to understand the importance of passing legislation like The CROWN Act at a national level.

Taking time to better understand the levels of culture that exist in our classrooms allows educators to forge deep and meaningful connections with the students and communities they serve. This process requires us to become students of our students and not mass reproducers of mainstream norms that disproportionally disregard students' cultural capital, especially students of color.

Batgirl

(Because Batman Can't Save Everyone)

"A student whose behavior pushes you away is a student who needs connection before anything else."
~ Hardcore Behaviorist

I could not tell this story without first explaining the context of my high school reality. Where I'm from, I learned one lesson very early on. When someone wants to fight you, you don't back down, and you never show fear. When folks grow up without a lot of money, toughness becomes a form of capital. It's the prerequisite to getting respect. Being a light-skinned girl with a petite frame made it even more imperative that my toughness not be questioned. When I was a sophomore in high school, I was on the junior varsity cheerleading squad. It had come to my attention that two disgruntled varsity cheerleaders were planning to jump me. Jumping a person is when two or more people simultaneously fight a person who is fighting alone.

For those unfamiliar with the severity of such a threat, I had seen girls annihilated when two or more females decided they were deserving of such a jumping. I'm not talking about a lightweight catfight; I'm talking about a queen-of-the-jungle-sabretooth-tiger fight where the head goes one way, and the uprooted weave goes the other way. These were the fights that bankrupt the victim's street credibility until they can fight the folks who jumped them individually and reclaim some ounce of dignity.

While I had girlfriends that would have my back in a fight, I still stood a chance of being jumped. For example, I could have been caught off guard by the two-person fight crew in the hallways between classes. For this reason, I decided I would carry a bat with me during the day at school. Dawn Rice was the newest assistant principal at our campus, and I hadn't had a chance to figure her out just yet. It was just my luck that the day I decided I would begin carrying Judge Judy (that's the name of the metal bat that still rides in the trunk of my SUV for safety purposes) from class to class, I ran into the newly hired administrator who clearly hadn't yet come to know who I was.

I was active on campus serving in the student council, cheering, and taking advanced courses by the time this threat was issued. As such, they typically let us involved students slide with minor offenses that the "regular kids" couldn't get away with. Rice hadn't received that memo. Approaching her duty post in the main hallway, I switched my bat to the outside hand furthest away from her (as if to conceal my weapon). Undeterred by my maneuver, she stopped me and questioned why I was carrying a bat in the hallways. Despite my best efforts to explain that I had recently taken up softball and was preparing to try out for the team, she confiscated my bat. I was furious! Where the administrator on my campus saw a lying teenager who might be a threat to other students, I was, in my mind, disarmed prey, now vulnerable to whatever attack the disgruntled varsity cheerleaders had waiting for me.

The next day, as I walked to class with another junior varsity cheerleader, we saw Rice posted in her usual duty spot. At this point, my friend was also unaware of who Rice was, so as we approached, I gave my friend the proper indirect introduction in one sentence,

"Yeah, that's the Bitch that took my bat," in a loud enough voice for the new administrator to know I had not forgotten her discretions. We both laughed as we sashayed on down the hallway in our cheer uniforms. Rice didn't say a word.

The following day in class, I received a notification that I had been assigned a week in In-School Suspension (ISS) due to the disrespect from the day before. "THE NERVE OF THAT BITCH! So, you take my bat, then place ME in ISS! I am STEPHANIE! I don't go to ISS! THE CAMPUS MISCREANTS GO THERE!" Yet there I was—all week. And placement in ISS also meant no cheering at the football game that week. I was sick, but it's safe to say after that encounter, I knew who Rice was, and she knew who I was.

After that unorthodox introduction, we built mutual respect. Rice ensured I knew there were consequences for my actions and held me to a higher standard that I couldn't talk myself out of. Before I graduated, I was a regular "Rice baby," who spent free time in her office and even worked as her office aid. After high school, she continued mentoring me, even writing my letter when I applied to join her sorority in college. And when I came back to teach in that same school years later, she loved to share the story of "Batgirl and The Day She Met Rice."

Chapter 3

The Proximity Principle

When it comes to cultural sensitivity, diversity/equity/inclusion/belonging, implicit bias, and all the other topics related to social justice, proximity is the missing puzzle piece that many schools, companies, and non-profits seek. When it comes to better understanding and connecting to groups of people with cultural differences, nothing gets to the heart of the matter like spending real time with real people. This is why segregation of the races has historically been such a necessary element in sustaining racial injustice. At our core, humans desire connection. Spending real time with any person or group of people inevitably leads to folks discovering what we have in common because we gain the opportunity to get past the apparent differences that typically exist at the surface.

Through housing discrimination and redlining, endogamy (restricting marriage between racial groups), segregated schools, social clubs and amenities, or occupational hierarchies, the framers and others, who worked to ensure separation and oppression of people of color, knew the farther away we were from each other, the more distrust and misunderstanding would exist between groups of people. For the sake of this book, we don't have time to deep-dive into the history of segregation in America. Most people can observe and acknowledge that much of our lives remain segregated decades after the Supreme Court ruled against segregation in 1954 and Congress passed the civil rights legislation in 1965, and even though most of the laws and policies that mandated race-based separation no longer exist.

While many folks like to talk about segregation as though it is a long-lost memory in the annals of time, the truth is I am a millennial and in the first generation of real integration. My father was the first Black man to graduate from an all-White high school in Texas. I believe it was the integration of schools that led to so many younger White people taking to the streets demanding justice and standing with Black folks in the Summer of 2020. Schools are sacred spaces for connection. I'm convinced that students of all colors, cultures, and races being in classes together, playing sports together, leading organizations together, and competing in academic competitions together has created more cause for shared concern about each other than reading a book about the other's experience. This sharing of space and understanding of the other fosters concern for each other's wellbeing as humans. This authentic connection is the heart of the proximity principle.

This proximity principle is why you can go into a school that serves students of color as a majority and see White teachers who can connect and get better outcomes than a Black and disconnected person. It's the reason diversity hires don't fix the problem. In the words of Angela Rye, "All skinfolk ain't kinfolk." This expression means that any person, regardless of race, doesn't share the same values as or necessarily have proximity to the neighborhood and culture of the students they serve. Proximity gets to the heart of the matter, and people making connections matters to the heart. For this reason, instructional leaders have to value and prioritize educators with connections to the communities in which their schools exist. Herein lies the challenge.

Some educators reading this will quickly push back here, now, at this spot, and for good reason. With a shortage of teachers, many leaders find it challenging to find quality applicants, and when they have found someone of quality (on paper at least), it is not easy to assess the candidate's cultural competence. Having spent many years in positions interviewing teachers and filling jobs, I understand that struggle. I am not overlooking this fact, but I think there are a few best practices we can use to hire, train, and retain educators on the importance of proximity and this work.

Performative Interviews

While this approach does require time and planning on the front end, it is invaluable when executed with fidelity. The idea here is to still have a tra-ditional sit-down interview followed by an interview where the teacher is required to create a lesson and teach it for a class of students in the actual school building. While it requires some preliminary legalities and consent forms on the front end, and there are limitations to be considered when a person has no relationships with the students, there are also some invaluable observations to be made when an applicant has to get into close proximity with your students. How do they speak to the students? Are they respectful? Do they create opportunities to include the student's interest? Do they center the students as learners during the lesson? Are they likable?

Although a one-time lesson is not the primary measure of what a teacher can do over time, performative interviewing allows educational leaders to see candidates in action. The icing on the cake comes with the evaluative survey responses provided by the students after experiencing the prospective teacher's lesson. The students are the experts in how effective the lesson is, after all.

Background Questions

Digging into a person's background and mindset will help you better glean where they stand on the proximity principle. I remember stalking the Dean of Instruction at the first high school that ever hired me to teach, Thurgood Marshall High School in Missouri City, Texas (shout out to the class of 2010). I would show up at the school and ask for a tour or ask to schedule an appointment with her or the principal; I would send them emails attaching my resume and expressing my interest in teaching at their campus.

Finally, being worn down by my persistent stalking, the Dean of Instruction met with me, and her first question was, "Why, out of all the schools have you set your sights, so intently, on working here?" I explained to her that I lived not too far from her campus, and I had thoroughly researched schools in the area and identified her campus and one other that served the demographic of students I'm called to serve. I expressed my understanding of the unique challenges that existed on her campus and my desire to serve because of those challenges. Eventually, she hired me. Not because I had experience

(I had none), not because of my degree (I was an alternative certification candidate with a psychology degree), not because of my network (I had no one to put in a good word for me), but because of my heart for the kids and the community.

Probing questions about where a person is from, why they think they are a good fit to teach at a specific campus, what they know about the demographics and the challenges that exist, why they are a good fit to address those challenges, what, if any, work they have done in that community or similar communities, or what is significant about the community. These types of questions redirect focus from the content and science of teaching (things we can professionally develop over time) to the heart and art of teaching (something we cannot singularly teach in professional development sessions). Give me an educator, young or old, with a heart for a community, and I can teach them pedagogy and curriculum and mentor them to use best instructional practices.

Community-Centered Professional Development

When new hires come in, they need to understand the campus's commitment to the community. I can't tell you how many schools I've been to that take on a them-versus-us ideology regarding the neighborhoods surrounding the schools. This ideology creates a culture clash that runs deep, especially within schools in communities of color. This clash is not simply about race, as many educators of color who are middle class in low-income schools also sometimes engage in similar ways as teachers who are racially different than their students. For this reason, professional development that emphasizes the cultural capital and value of the community is as essential for the new hires as pedagogy training.

In affluent areas, the value of the community is ever-present. When an educator even hints at wanting to devalue any aspect of the community, its members and students' parents show up and demand changes and ensure their voices are heard. They expect that the community school they send their tax dollars to works for them and their kids. Period. In communities where people have historically experienced the sting of marginalization, some people come to develop a deep distrust for what they understand to be another system perpetuating war against their communities. It is up to the school to act swiftly and explicitly when ensuring their community connections are not only listed in the texts of statements mounted on walls in buildings but also are embroidered in the very culture of the campus. Teachers know the difference.

Community Connections

As a principal, I required teachers to build a community connection to each unit they taught during the school year. I'll go into more detail and provide explanations and pictures in the Higher Order section to come. In essence, what it says is that teachers have to curate learning opportunities that invite the community into classrooms and students into the community. No matter what content a teacher is teaching, the state created that curriculum, allegedly (let's not debate that today), to prepare students to be upstanding, knowledgeable citizens of society and benefit the workforce. Ok. If that is the case, then the knowledge and skills you are teaching kids in your classroom are already being leveraged in society. I asked teachers to get very explicit in connecting the folks whose work or practice utilized that knowledge and skills daily.

Again, there are more examples of those connections later in the book. However, requiring teachers to foster these relationships is necessary to create real-world connections for students and to show the community members that they are valued and welcomed in the schools. Many people and companies will jump at the opportunity to come into schools for live demonstrations, experiments, donations of resources, expert talks, judges for presentations, etc. They are just waiting for the opportunity for a good photo-op with those kiddos to show they are giving back to local schools. Educators can only leverage the community when they have clarity about how to engage with the community effectively.

Cultural Plunges

In a class on race and education, one assignment we completed was a cultural plunge. Our professor challenged us to go out and have a social experience with a group of people who were racially different than us. Another Black classmate and I decided we would meet two of our White cohort members at a dance hall they were familiar with called the Red River Saloon. Yes, a saloon! If there is one place a Black girl from the hood isn't used to culturally, it's a honky-tonk country music hall fully equipped with a mechanical bull. But there I was, poised for a cultural plunge.

In my mind, I had a perfect sense that this would be like a scene out of one of those black-and-white television western shows where a person entering the saloon pushes open those two wooden doors, which slowly creek open, and the music screeches to a halt. I expected everyone would turn and dart their eyes at my forehead as if to ask, "Who let Black folks into the saloon?" followed by God knows what else. This is the stereotype, I held in my mind's eye for White people who went to a place called a saloon. Imagine my surprise when we got to the saloon and were not only let in without incident but also welcomed. There were actually other Black people on the dance floor, and they even played some songs by Black artists. And the kicker was the older White fellow that took a liking to my plunge partner and spent the evening dancing with us. We had a hot, sweaty, cranberry-vodka filled, do-si-doing, good ole time.

That is the power of a cultural plunge. I'd argue that many districts could benefit from having teachers plunge into the social spaces of their communities on some of those Professional Development days instead of sitting in a room learning about cultural sensitivity isolated within the four walls of the campus buildings where they presume themselves safe from the "dangerous neighborhood hoodlums." Let them have immersive experiences attending a Sunday church service, going to a community YMCA, or--my personal favorite—sitting in a barber or beauty shop during business hours.

Expressing the objective of these visits to business owners and leaders in the community would create all kinds of authentic partnerships that move past the contrived "one night in the community" photo opportunity initiatives and toward cultivating deep, rich relationships. I challenge educators everywhere I go to take a plunge and experience the culture of the other. Yet after I leave, many go back to doing the daily tasks of "business as usual." This is why I press educational leaders to make these types of initiatives a priority and make them more fun and exploratory rather than mandatory and evaluative. The possibilities are endless.

While I could go on and on about the power of the proximity principle (the main focus of my next book 😄), I'll end by saying, "give it a shot." If you make a more pointed effort to get into proximity with the community you serve and nothing changes, then you've lost nothing. Yet, if I'm right, you can gain so much from this level of deep, rich connecting and learning!

References and Resources

Apple, M. W. (1995). *Education and Power*. Routledge.

Diangelo, R. (2018). *White fragility*. Beacon Press.

Dweck, C. S. (2008). *Mindset the New Psychology of Success*. Ballantine.

Emdin, C. (2016). *For White Folks Who Teach in the Hood – and the Rest of Y'all Too: Reality Pedagogy and Urban Education*. Beacon Press.

Hammond, Z. L. (2015). *Culturally Responsive Teaching and the Brain*. Corwin Press.

Lee & Low Books. (2020). *Where is the Diversity in Publishing? The 2019 Diversity Baseline Survey Results*. https://blog.leeandlow.com/2020/01/28/2019diversity-baselinesurvey/

Pierson, R.F. (2013, May). *Every Kid Needs a Champion*. TED Talks Education. https://www.ted.com/talks/rita_pierson_every_kid_needs_a_champion/details?language=en

Singh, A. (2019). *The Racial Healing Handbook*. New Harbinger Publications.

Villanueva, E. (2018). *Decolonizing Wealth: Indigenous Wisdom to Heal Divides and Restore Balance*. Berrett-Koehler Publishers.

Wilkerson, I. (2020). *Caste*. Random House.

Yosso, T. (2005). *Whose culture has capital? A critical race theory discussion of community cultural wealth. Race Ethnicity and Education, 8*(1), 69-91. https://www.iirp.edu/images/pdf/AvNtDE_EDUC_701_-_Yossos_Community_Cultural_Wealth_Model.pdf

PART II

The F.R.E.S.H. Classroom Approach

Bus Fight

(Because street cred is important)

After 5th grade, my mom and I (yes, it was a team effort) were divorcing her husband. While I was more than excited to be getting away from her uber-controlling, narcissistic companion for good, I was completely distraught about the idea of being forced to move to a new city and start the new school cycle all over again (by the end of K-12, I had attended 10 different campuses in 6 different school districts... exhausting). My mom always attempted to cushion the blow of our upcoming migration by reassuring me that, because I was so great at meeting new friends and people loved me, I would be fine. Nevertheless, I was devastated.

I still remember my 5th-grade smart mouth attempting to explain to her why the current district was so much stronger academically than the new district and how detrimental that would be to my learning. Yet, I still ended up in the city of Lancaster, TX, and it was an anomaly. It was geographically a southern suburb of Dallas, TX, but it was an urban-characteristic area in many regards. In my mind, it was kind of like an overflow from its northern neighbor Oak Cliff, a southern region in the City of Dallas, TX. The demographics had been rapidly changing, and the schools were majority African American by the time I began school there.

I started 6th grade at the district's Sixth Grade Center, and I learned one thing real fast: This place was different. It was tough. Many of the students were more mature. Their conversations were a lot coarser than those by the students at the school I'd come from. As you may imagine, it didn't take long for me to be challenged to my first school fight. Perhaps I had a chip on my shoulder as the new girl in a new town I despised. Perhaps it was because a cute new girl getting too much attention from the boys was a challenge to some pre-existing social order that was unknown to me. Whatever the reason, a rumor started to spread that one girl (I'll call her T) was telling our classmates she was going to fight me. To this day, I have no clue if this threat was real or contrived in the depraved mind of a classmate looking for entertainment. Either way, word of this threat hit the campus, and it was a defining moment for me. Fight or flight. Sink or swim. Stand up or get knocked down.

Now that your interest is peaked, awaiting the school bus showdown's juicy details, let me tell you one thing. Some of your students do not want to fight. Many students with a big bark would love for someone to throw them a lifeline and give them a cop-out that doesn't look like weakness or backing down. I would have loved for an adult to have intercepted this threat, brought us into a restorative circle with the counselor, and let us get to the bottom of resolving our issue without violence and foolery.

This is why as an administrator I tried, as often as I was permitted, to implement restorative practices on campuses. I've seen the power those circles have to allow students and parents on opposing ends of an issue to stop and see the humanity in the other. I've seen the power of communication as a tool to de-escalate a brewing disagreement and teach kids effective alternatives to conflict resolution. This power is why I'll always advocate for restorative discipline in schools. But there was no intervention, no restorative circles to curb altercations, no saving me. I had to fight.

In order for this fight to happen I had to get on T's bus (I was a walker). This bus would, in fact, be going the opposite direction of my apartment, but it was necessary to meet this threat head on. If not, it would be a clear sign to other students that I was weak, a punk, open for others to challenge and harass. So, I got on the bus.

The first stretch of this bus ride went without incident, and as we neared the stop where I would have to get off, I knew it was now or never. I made my way to the center aisle, which was all I had to do for all the messy observers to get T into the aisle as well. After little to no verbal exchanges we were a flailing ball of wind milling, hairpulling fools. All these years later, all I remember is that the punches started flying, and when they stopped, I was on top of T, one hand full of microwave ponytail curls and the other hand throwing blind punches, as she struggled to get up.

At some point, someone intervened pulling me off T. Afterwards I scurried off the bus — adrenaline racing, heart pumping wildly — only to realize my nose was bleeding. I had been unaware that any part of my body was hurting at all due to the crazed rush of energy that sent us crashing around on that bus like we were demon possessed. I made my way home to nurse my wounds and conceal any manner of this foolishness from my mother (she was not tolerant of such ratchetness).

Over the years, I participated in other fights for the same reason, to prove I was no punk. In my years as an educator, I oftentimes interjected myself and played mediator when I heard through the grapevine that some of my students were beefing or ready to fight. I know how it feels to be called out and feel afraid to back down for fear of future threats. Because of that experience, I have tried to be a voice of reason and allow myself to be the out so two kids wouldn't fight. In the end, that's the lesson the bus fight taught me.

Chapter 4

CRSB - Culturally Responsive, Standards-Based Teaching

In their 2011 book entitled, *Culturally Responsive Standards-Based Teaching: Classroom to Community and Back*, Saifer et al. lay the groundwork from which I built the FRESH approach. They wrote: "CRSB teaching is the integration of two important aspects of education: culturally responsive teaching and standards-based teaching... [that] values students' culture, draws on that culture as a strength in their education, and challenges them with a rigorous, relevant curriculum." The emphasis here is the explicit valuing of the cultural capital students possess while also holding the expectation of academic achievement high for all students.

In our FRESH Workshops, I use the graphic below to illustrate CRSB to educators.

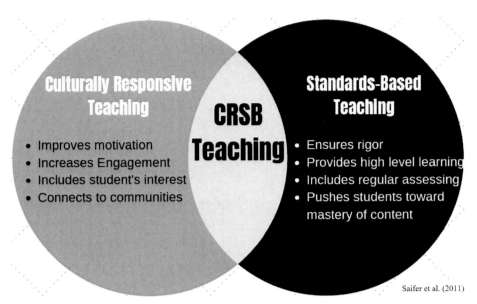

Saifer et al. (2011)

This Venn diagram helps educators better understand both parts of this equation. Often, educators receive professional development about all things related to standards-based teaching, from formative assessments to analyzing content standards. Rarely, if ever, are teachers receiving quality, ongoing professional development and coaching around understanding the cultural capital students possess and how to embed that cultural understanding into the instructional experiences they craft daily.

I would be remiss not to pause here to acknowledge the countless number of researchers contributing to this field of study over the years, most notably the OGs of Culturally Relevant Pedagogy, namely Gloria Ladson-Billings, and Culturally Responsive Teaching, namely Geneva Gay. While it would be cliché to say I stand on the shoulders of these and many other giants in the field, there is no denying that their commitment to this work has given us much insight into best practices for decades.

Instructional Modalities

In 2020, the COVID pandemic found many educators and campuses diving headfirst into online learning at warp speed. Straight away, many people who were habitually committed to traditional teaching practices found that their teacher-centered attempts at virtual teaching fell flat. Internet memes of half-snoozing students slumped down in front of computer screens with classmates laughingly looking on regularly circulated throughout all the social media channels. While these images may have provided some much-needed comic relief during a difficult time, students' attendance and attrition during the online distance learning periods created a national crisis among educators.

When we resumed our FRESH Workshops, we had both a live virtual training and a self-paced digital course. While I was aware that people were being pushed to the brink of professional insanity and looking for a lifeline, the truth was CRSB was still the lifeline. I found ways to repackage and distribute the workshop mid-pandemic because I understood, as did all the researchers and authors that came before me that the key is to always lean into centering on our students. Even when the delivery went from in-person to virtual learning, we knew of ways to engage our students with intriguing dialogue and debates, incorporating household items into lesson activities, web-based games and quizzes, and so much more.

One of my dearest friends, TaMichael Bassett, was an elementary school teacher. We talk about all-things education weekly, and I had to pause here to say that this pandemic found her, like many of you, trying new things. I remember calling her one day and finding her in the midst of conducting home visits for students who had gone MIA. I was floored by how her heart for her students and determination to engage them drove her outside the four walls of her school building and into the community to connect with those little learners.

I'm not one of those people who glamorizes overworking and not having a work-life balance. I am an advocate for working smarter during the workday. Seeing so many educators find creative ways to get into the community to connect with students was a blessing. From drive-by parades to drive-thru food pick-up points, to personalized graduation yard signs, and through-the-window home visits, many educators refused to retreat when faced with the myriad complications of implementing virtual learning.

In a time of grave uncertainty, teachers did what they always do: They showed up and got shit done! Pat yourself on the back if you were teaching during the pandemic. As a matter of fact, turn up a glass of something stiff in celebration of yourself (if you're into that sort of relaxation). You navigated through one of the toughest challenges our profession has ever experienced collectively. No matter how many instructional wins or loses you endured in the process, you can only go up from here. So, Are You Ready to Get FRESH?

DAEP Sentencing

(Because middle school is tough, man)

While in-school suspension (ISS) was harsh, nothing sucked worse than District Alternative Education Placement (DAEP). I was "sentenced" to alternative school placements twice during middle school. Once for fighting, and once for having way too many referrals. I was a repeat offender. So, imagine how surprised parents and students were when I disclosed that to them in my office before issuing them a DAEP placement.

I've had students sitting in my office wide-eyed in disbelief and confused about how it's possible that their administrator could have ever been convicted of similarly heinous acts. The truth is it's the struggles of my childhood journey that led me to become a better educator. When some people label certain students "bad," I take that personally. I like to tell students, "There are no bad kids, only bad choices, so choose to be great!" It's all a choice!

A child can go from making terrible choices that lead to multiple DAEP placements (hello somebody!) to becoming a student leader, cheer captain, prom queen, and first-generation college student (toot, toot). But only educators can change the conversation from "What is wrong with this bad kid?" to "What is causing this kid to make such bad choices?" The former question is easy, as it places the weight of the responsibility on the kid and often the parents. The second question requires educators to think in deep and meaningful ways about the why behind the what?

No matter how many bad choices I managed to make during those troubled years, my mother always reminded me I was not a bad kid. I was a child of God.

I'm sure the maturity of aging naturally played a part in my evolution but getting involved in sports and organizations also helped me so much. Group and team memberships raised the stakes. Whereas a trip to ISS or DAEP may have fewer implications for an independent student disconnected from the school community, a student with more to lose will second guess sacrificing participation and team time for a random fight with a hater. A student having to sit out the week of a big game they've been preparing for months and letting down their team is a big deal. It makes students have to step up their decision-making game quickly.

But isn't that life? Isn't it true that the more time, money, and energy we invest in degrees, certifications, jobs, kids, spouses, businesses, the less likely we are to act a fool and risk it all (in the case of most mentally balanced adults)? For instance, some car dips in front of you to steal the parking spot you've been waiting on for 5 minutes. The next thing you know, you're seeing red and ready to cuss. You could hop out of the car and slap on that person's window, giving them a piece of your mind until they get out and engage you in a ratchet parking-lot brawl. Or you could hurl a smart-mouthed retort at your front windshield for only you and God to hear and speed off to stay jail-free another day. The more we have to lose, the less likely we are to engage in foolery.

It is typically in the absence of resources and opportunities that people are willing to risk it all and wild out. For that reason, I always encourage campus leaders to provide all the extracurricular activities and organizations possible. Seriously, max out! As a principal, every teacher at my school had to sponsor a sports team or organization. Think about the possibilities the STEM club, dance team, cheer team, volleyball, basketball, football, student government, book club, girls/boys mentorship groups, environmental club, Anime club, chess club, academic decathlon, poetry club, math club, etc. that allow students to invest time and energy that supports making good choices. The more you can appeal to students' interests and get them plugged into the school community, the more they will experience a sense of belonging and accountability to those looking forward to seeing them show up.

You do realize that's what happens with students who get connected with gangs in neighborhoods, right? Acceptance, belonging, productivity, accountability, family. While students may have ISS or DAEP placements, they need to get plugged in when they come back to the campus community ready for redemption.

They need another chance. What you offer them can be the difference between their evolution or commitment to more of the same.

Chapter 5

F.R.E.S.H. Classroom Approach

Fun, Relevant, Engaging, Standards-Based, and Higher Order

The F.R.E.S.H. acronym stands for Fun, Relevant, Engaging, Standards-Based, and Higher Order (FRESH). After years of being a student in under-resourced communities with students of color, then teaching and leading in the same kinds of schools, traveling across the country, visiting schools in similar communities that were creating success with students, and conducting and analyzing scholarly research in similar schools, these five areas emerged as the most practical aspects of the successes I observed. From Atlanta to Washington, DC, to the South Side of Chicago, to Dallas, as well as other cities, I have delighted in going into schools that work (an intentional contrast to research that focuses solely on why schools don't work for students of color and other deficit approaches). I conduct class observations, interview teachers and principals, talk to students, and look into data. I don't believe any school's success can be fully understood by only reviewing test scores, so my approach is a little more holistic.

After years of reading literature and hearing from trainers more focused on the theoretical than the practical, I created the FRESH approach, as I believe that teachers need actionable, practical strategies that can, when implemented with fidelity, help them maximize their classroom instruction. This is my offering to you. Let's dive in.

Chapter 6

F = FUN

Fun needs no introduction. No matter what your idea of fun is (shopping, riding a motorcycle, running marathons, quilting, dancing the night away), one thing is universally true about fun. It is consuming! No matter what language a person is speaking, you know the look of fun when you see it.

Often conversations about education are specifically focused on students and what's best for them. Although this is always the best place to start a conversation, the truth of the matter is that teaching is your profession! It's your livelihood! I mean, who wakes up and says, "I can't wait to get to work so that I can teach these standards that someone deemed necessary for kids to learn to become contributing members of society! YES!" No teacher I've ever met in the field.

The truth is we do it for the kids, but the idea of creating fun classrooms for kids means fun work environments for adults. Who doesn't like to have fun? Who's ever knowingly avoided fun under normal circumstances? People are drawn to things that are fun to them. How else can you explain a mud run? People are actually paying to run in mud and enjoying two things I abhor: cardio and filth. 😂 🧟

I argue that fun campuses and classrooms are beneficial for students AND teachers. When I was teaching, nothing got me as hyped for the day as knowing that I had a killer lesson prepped. It motivated me! I made it a common practice to lay out everything I would need for the next day's lesson before

I left to go home each day (Most days at least. Not going to catch me in the early morning copy room race for the regularly jammed copy machine). 😂

While every lesson will not be a pulse-pounding funfest, fun activities and moments are characteristic of a FRESH classroom. Sometimes, students have a test to take or a writing assignment that requires quiet, but more times than that, teachers and students should have some fun!

HOW DO I MAKE MY TEACHING FUN?

Someone reading right now is thinking *they pay me to teach these standards; they don't pay me to make it fun* (Bless those students' hearts). However, someone else is thinking *I would love to have more fun, but I just don't know how*. For you, my newfound friend, I have the following things you could commit to doing tomorrow! Let's go!

Music Make You Lose Control 💃

Insert Missy Elliot gyration

Much research has been done on the effects of using music in classrooms (you should trust me by now; I'm not citing 100 sources in this chapter). 😂 Music is major. If you've ever been to a party, sporting event, or even shopping in a store, music sets the tone. A smooth jazz instrumental on the elevator or a blaring dance track at a wedding reception, music is the pulse of our lives, and students these days consume a steady stream of music like never before.

In his hip-hop themed book, *MC Means Move the Class*, Dr. Shaun Woodly breaks down the symbiotic relationship that exist between teachers and DJs. Being both an educator and popular DJ, Dr. Woodly helps educators understand:

> The DJ with two turntables and a mic is a one-person powerhouse whose role is to transform a collection of songs in a crate to an engaging, next-level, cosmic experience for the audience. With this collection of songs... The DJ has to be a master of quite a few different elements to create an ideal experience. We're talking about song

selection, blending, transitions, timing, adjusting levels, matching themes, reading and responding to behavior patterns, and knowing the audience well enough to know what to say and what to play at all times and in real time.

Just the same, a well-equipped educator is also a one-person powerhouse whose role is to transform a collection of learning objectives and lessons into an engaging, next-level, cosmic experience for their students. With this content expertise, it is simply not a matter of getting students to memorize information and terms one after the other. The teacher has to be a master of quite a few different elements to create an ideal experience.

A source of stimulation in a one-to-many environment, both the DJ and teacher are artists.

In the spirit of moving the crowd in your classroom, here are three ways I managed to effectively use music in the classroom that I believe can assist teachers in facilitating fun and creating good vibes for all.

Classroom Management

No matter the subject matter, you can use music to manage your campus and/or classroom. A few years back, in a video of New Manchester High School in Douglasville, Ga., the transition bells were replaced by a 5-minute music track. Instead of a shouting bell signaling the end of class, student-created musical tracks invited students into the hallways to transition. How dope is that?

In the same tune, I used gospel/inspirational music first thing in the morning to help transition my own mind to the start of another day. Then, as my students arrived and worked through the bellringer, I let the music play quietly in the background. When the music stopped, they knew to wrap up that sentence and get ready to transition to the next thing. In the morning, some students would stop by my room to hear a little gospel music before they went to their first-period class because some students, like Alexus, expressed they just "needed a little Jesus before going to class." 😄 After lunch, I would often put on some soothing music to help myself and my students as we refocused and got back to work (they clearly overdose on sugar in the cafeteria and wild out). When I was rushing and didn't turn the music on, students would request I play the music.

As a principal, I encouraged my teachers to incorporate music during class, and I often would hear smooth tunes crooning when students were working in small groups. When the music turned off, students knew it was time to transition to the next small-group station. I reinforced this practice with my teachers when facilitating their professional development weekly meetings. I set the tone with instrumental-only jazz (as they were just coming out of busy classrooms) while they worked through PLC activities.

Lyrical Analysis

In addition to the sound of music, the lyrics of songs your students listen to have power in your classroom as well. If you want to learn a lot about the students you serve, relate the content of some of their favorite songs to what you will be doing in class. During a poetry unit, I constructed small group stations that contained song lyrics to an older song and a contemporary one that was thematically connected. Students had to evaluate the lyrics to both pieces and identify the universal theme that emerged. Lastly, they compared and contrasted the different poetic elements used by the writers and constructed a short answer response based on their findings.

During a unit on Beowulf, English IV students analyzed different parts of the story. Then they selected one piece that was meaningful to them and created CDs (clearly a thing of the past; these days, a YouTube playlist would suffice) with songs they felt embodied the tone and mood that the author conveyed in that section of the story. Students were given a corresponding writing assignment that allowed them to articulate the selection process for their songs and the connections they made.

In another lesson, I posted lyrics from a verse in a rap song by Drake and made students identify and analyze his use of similes and metaphors. While students were rambling off the lyrics as they pumped through their headphones in the hallways daily, many of them had not taken the time to analyze what the rapper was actually saying about himself and his experiences as he utilized figurative language in many of his songs. The truth is good writing is the origin of many things we love and consume daily (i.e., movies, songs, newscasts, sitcoms, plays, etc.). I just needed to connect those lyrics to the students who appreciated them.

The Remix

Teachers also have the option of remixing or allowing students to remix songs of various musical genres for the sake of remembering and/or getting familiar with instructional content. The term remixing, in this context, means to take the track of the music of a popular song and change the lyrics. If you're anything like me, you learned your alphabet to the melody of what we now commonly refer to as The Alphabet Song. All these years later, I often recall that melody when I am completing a task that requires me to place documents in alpha order. While we don't use this technique to remember everything (we'd be singing all day), adding a melody to some things students just have to remember is a tool that aids FRESH teachers. Below is a remix activity I used in the classroom.

Freestyle Friday was an activity I used to help students review for vocabulary tests on Fridays. To prep for this activity, I wrote down one of the 10 vocabulary words on different index cards. As students walked into class, I randomly passed 10 kids a different word for the week. After the bellringer, when it was time to review for the test, the "volun-told" students who received a card would come to the front and prepare to freestyle. A random student from the class would provide us a beat (knocking and tapping atop the desk), and we would take turns listening to each student spit their two-line raps where they were required to use the vocabulary term in the proper context. Of course, some students would be mortified, and they did have the choice to pass their word off to another student if they wanted, but I also got involved by freestyling myself (cheat code: If I created a rap using one word, I'd use the same rap all day). 😂 🎤

Games and Competitions

Nothing is more fun than a good ole game! Competition not only makes

America thrive but, in a safe environment, it can also make a classroom pretty fun! Create or look up "games students can play in small groups or whole groups" that cover the content for the day while getting students immersed in a game-like environment.

As an assistant principal, I can recall hosting a math relay with a group of elementary students. Using index cards, I wrote addition and subtraction questions on the front of each card for students to see. On the back, I wrote the answer for me to see. Two teams played the game split into two lines facing me. I held up the math problem, and the first student who guessed the answer earned a point for their team. The student who did not guess the answer first went over to the "sidelines" where their teacher was located with sidewalk chalk to walk them through solving the problem. We wanted to be sure that the student who didn't guess the answer first had a chance to show they knew how to solve the problem or receive a real-time intervention. The following two kiddos in line stepped up for their math problem, and the game continued until we covered all the math problems.

Students, teachers, and even I, as the administrator, had a blast during math relays! Reviewing math problems at the end of the unit could have been less fun with a worksheet while students sat quietly facing the front of the room, but with just a little more time and creative thinking, we had astronomical levels of fun!

If you are a teacher who feels like you just aren't creative enough to think of your own games and competitions, I have news that will make your day so much brighter! Google. You can search for games as broad as math games and down to specific skills like addition games. Sites like Teachers Pay Teachers and Pinterest are sure to provide you with more ideas than one teacher could ever use. Don't beat yourself up if you don't think you're creative enough to come up with things because there is no power in recreating the wheel! Somebody already set you up for success! Just don't forget to adapt what you find to fit the needs and interest of YOUR students.

Be Flexible

Relinquish the idea that you need to control every second of every moving moment in the classroom. The truth is fun teachers know how to be flexible. Flexible doesn't refer to the class where students are yelling and bouncing off the walls with no instructional direction (God, no). Flexibility, in this context, refers to a teacher's ability to give students wiggle room and choices. Do all students have to sit at their desks during independent practice, pencils perched perfectly in hand? I argue no. Will students sitting on the floor, bean bag, or standing as they work on an activity cause chaos and burn the school to the ground? Usually not. Is Jimmy standing in the back as he works disturbing anyone outside of you and your need to have all students sitting up straight in rows in alphabetical order? Usually not.

As the principal of an intermediate school, I remember encountering a particularly entertaining student; I will call him Derek. Derek was your classic case of a class clown on a mission to capitalize on any opportunity to interject an uninvited punchline into any classroom scenario. I must admit, he was masterful with his timing, facial expressions, and delivery. He was our resident comedian. Time and time again, I can recall famous comedians reflecting on their time in K-12 classrooms and their ongoing clashes with teachers and administrators fighting to keep them "in line." I resolved not to let that be our story. Instead, we found ways to foster Derek's comedic genius by honing it and allowing him to have the spotlight when it was appropriate for his comedic performances.

One such instance was during the school talent showcase. While speaking with students about what they were planning to present, Derek told me he would be in the audience because he didn't have a talent. The SAME student I just described with the perfect comedic timing didn't even realize he had an opportunity to let his gift shine, but I did. I brought Derek into my office and sat him down. I explained to him that, as the resident comedian, he had to showcase his skills. I made myself available for him to stop by my office for the next week as he prepared to bounce material off of me, and I made sure he understood the importance of being respectful to students and faculty.

On the day of the talent show, Derek was nervous, but I knew he would be ok because I saw in him the same thing I see in Kevin Hart, Dave Chappell, and many other great comedians. He had that IT factor. As Derek took the stage, he was visibly nervous but flashed that contagious smile as all his classmates clapped; they were eager to see, what would be, the only standup comedy act of the day. He started in, warming the jokes up, and then he really got going and went into his jokes about the math teacher (notorious for assigning copious amounts of homework), asking the audience, "And what's up with Mr. McNeal and this homework?" as he let the mic drop to his side and rolled his eyes in complete disgust. The students erupted in thunderous applause, hurling their "Amens" and affirming words at the altar of his comedic connection. By the end of the act, every person in the room was on their feet, and the students rushed the stage to hug Derek for actually doing it! And Derek, yes, he was beaming. He was shining. He was affirmed.

Listen to kids and consider their suggestions. As a principal, students knew I had an open-door policy, and the school was theirs, so their opinions could change things the same way their parent's views could. This consideration and inclusion is no different in the classroom. FRESH teachers stay in the habit of assessing their own practices through informal and formal student assessments. When's the last time you asked kids what they thought about your class? Ways you could make the class more fun for them? They'll tell you!

Oftentimes we survey parents and seek to understand their expectations, while students (not parents) are the ones spending hours in our classrooms. Crazy. While I do not mean to devalue parental input, students are stakeholders too. Flexibility means having your classroom expectations but engaging in collaborative norm-making with students that include student behaviors and student input on their instructional expectations for the school year.

*Random side rant on the topic of flexibility. After working in elementary, intermediate, middle, high school, and higher ed and experiencing both the public and private sectors, let me say this. I HATE SINGLE-FILE LINES! Lines to get into the lunch line because we can only be served one at a time are okay. Lines because we are waiting for the restroom are okay. But my pet peeve is an overly rigid teacher yelling down the hallway for everyone to get in a single-file line like students are on a chain gang.

If the goal of education is to prepare students for the future, then let's do that. People do not naturally transition from place to place in straight lines. We naturally merge into single-filed lines when necessary as socially inclined human beings. What if we just taught kids to do normal social transitioning like walk to the right and use inside voices in the hallways as they naturally... just... walk? And don't get me started on bubbles in the mouth. 😐

Perhaps coming from high schools into elementary schools caused the disdain I feel for single-file lines, but now it is my biggest pet peeve. So, everyone, just stop it! (All of the elementary teachers are no longer interested in reading further. Please continue reading, as that rant is over, and it only gets better from here, I promise.) 😂

FRESH Lesson Planning Questions:

1. Where will I intentionally incorporate fun in the lessons for next week?
2. Which long-term competition is underway? Which short-term competition(s) will students engage in next week?
3. What various music channels on my streaming service are appropriate and intriguing to my students?
4. How will I assess my students to gain suggestions they have for making our class more fun?

Daddy Lessons

(Because Beyoncé isn't the only one with a tough dad)

My dad is the hardest working man I know. Even though he's well past retirement age now and could live well without working, he still works 7 days a week. Needless to say, my dad is built Ford tough (a thoroughbred is what he calls it). To this day, my father remains one of my biggest teachers, as our relationship has grown stronger with time, and I've come to understand better how his mind works. I believe Black people in his generation to be one of the most misunderstood groups of people. I'd like to share why I say that and what I think educators can take away from what I've learned.

While people like to think about Jim Crow laws as being some far-off part of America's dark past, my father was the first Black man to graduate from an all-White high school. To this day, when we drive through that town, he shows me the route Black people had to take to get into the government building using the back door marked with a "Colored" sign. He tells me about how his classmates respected him and other Black men at the time when their athletic prowess brought power to their sports programs. While Black athletes were valued for the muscle and speed they delivered to their teams, only White players could lead the teams during those times.

My father tells me all the good afforded to him by attending a White high school where students were learning to be business leaders and entrepreneurs instead of the Black school where students were being prepared to become workers. I can see how these lessons prepared him to be in business (he's been an entrepreneur my entire life). But on the other side of that coin, I understand the trauma he and other Black people were subjected to at the whims of some White people. One of the most terrifying examples of such terror came when my father found himself with the cold steel of a shotgun pressed into his side as a drunken White man threatened the lives of him and his friends. Their offense? Playing basketball in a gym when the terrorist decided they were no longer welcome.

I imagine that the external threats faced outside the home, coupled with the standard and sometimes extreme practice of corporal punishment that characterized many Black homes during that time, must have been a lot to navigate. I believe the survival and success of Black people of that generation required a certain amount of cognitive dissonance my peers and I will never fully understand. Where some may see them as emotionally disconnected, I've come to see their dispositions as necessary to survive and thrive in the world they inherited.

Having this understanding helped me extend grace to my father and to the parents I encountered in schools. Many of us will project our own expectations of what a "loving parent" should and shouldn't do in partnership with schools based on our personal upbringings. But I understand that most parents are doing the best they can with what they have. Instead of maintaining limited avenues for parental inclusion (i.e., PTA participation and field trip chaperoning), many schools can profit significantly by asking parents how they might contribute to the school community.

The possibilities are endless when we open our minds and hearts to others who "show up" differently than we expect. For example, one of my father's businesses is a unisex salon. While he may not have been the father to come to a PTA meeting, he may have been able to host an event before the new school year for students, in need, to get free haircuts and styles during the back-to-school rush. This way of showing up would be unique to my father and others in an industry like his, but it would take educators connecting to parents and tapping into what they have to offer because every parent/guardian has something to offer.

Added bonus: Below, I have included some Daddy Lessons I've accumulated from my dad over the years. Some of these may apply in educational settings. Some lessons are just for life. Enjoy!

- ✓ *Either run with the big dogs or stay on the porch. (Translation: Some people get in the ring and do things, others observe from the comfort of the sidelines.)*

- ✓ *The whole world will step aside for a person that knows where they're going. (Translation: When you pursue you purpose with boldness, people can't stop you from getting where you're going.)*

- ✓ *The best thing a job is for is to save enough money to start your own business. (Translation: Learn what you need to, then apply those lessons to starting your own business.)*

- ✓ *Before you go shooting off your big mouth, make sure your brain is loaded. (Translation: Be sure you've done your research and know the facts before you start talking.)*

- ✓ *When you own your businesses, no one tells you where to go and what to do. (Translation: Entrepreneurship gives you autonomy over your life.)*

- ✓ *When you make money, let your money go to work for you. Whether I go to work today or not, my money is making money for me. (Translation: Ownership of income-generating assets gives you financial freedom and residual income.)*

- ✓ *This is the hood, Stephanie. (Translation: Don't get so far removed that you forget how to connect with folks in the neighborhood.)*

- ✓ *If I had given you everything, you wouldn't have worked as hard. (Translation: You busted your butt to get your assets the way I had to bust my butt to get mine. And it made you stronger.)*

Chapter 7

R = Relevant

Making teaching relevant to students is largely contingent upon authentic teacher-student relationships. I've heard it said this way: Kids need to know we care before they care about what we know. While some students will come in, sit down, and learn whatever is put in front of them, FRESH teachers know that transformative teaching is incubated in a warm and caring environment. This is not to be mistaken with a mushy, feelings-driven environment (I have never been the mushy type). Caring doesn't mean relaxing standards, hosting pity parties, and providing participation trophies to everyone.

On the contrary, this type of caring deals with connecting with students and maintaining high expectations with their needs in mind. In my mind, there should be no other way. If you think of teachers as public servants employed by tax-paying citizens to teach their kids, then the standard of customer care and service should reflect that understanding. Some educators approach kids with a "this-is-my-classroom" approach, which couldn't be further from the truth.

The truth is educators can get off work and drive down the highway to a different community that they call home, while the students in community schools remain in the same neighborhoods. Educators can take jobs in school districts they choose, while the students and families stay inside the same communities that house their schools. Shared ownership should be mutual between educators and students and communities. For that reason, teachers should seek to understand their students and their students' communities the way Facebook's newsfeed algorithm aims to understand consumer behavior (Google that algorithm when you get a chance).

Teachers need to know: What are students into right now? What's happening in the neighborhood? If teachers don't know, they miss out on incredible opportunities to dig in and connect the content standards to the real world surrounding their students.

I can still remember one of my most impactful lessons in an English I class. In national news, a teen boy had recently been beaten to death in a gang fight on the South Side of Chicago, and I was going to use a related news article in class the next day, but I asked myself the question, "How could my students connect to this issue?" I didn't believe gang violence to be a problem in the community where I was working, but I knew students had their informal versions of gangs called "cliques" that they associated with. After class that day, I asked one of my student informants (I'll teach you more about recruiting informants later) to stay behind, and I asked her for the names of the cliques students associated with at our school. I then used the names of those groups in the bellringer students responded to the following day.

I wish I could tell you the looks of surprise and, in some cases, embarrassment as some students saw the names of their "cliques" splashed across the screen in class. They asked how I knew about these groups and probed me to determine what else I'd learned about their out-of-school engagements. I always fiercely reassured them I was all-knowing and omnipresent (I'd never give up my informants). LOL. This bellringer allowed students to reflect deeply about their own behaviors and affiliations before assigning them a reading and writing task to connect them to another situation across the country.

While the people who author your district-adopted textbooks are competent professionals and are very invested in creating helpful resources, they don't know your students. Students need you to bridge the otherwise irrelevant content and the realities of their lived experiences. Let's talk about how.

HOW DO I MAKE MY TEACHING RELEVANT?

Face the Truth

If you think about the things that interest you, you may have to face the fact that your students may consider those things a major snooze fest. If you are a teacher, you are more than likely, at least, middle-class, college-educated, middle-aged, and professional. On the other hand, some of your students may be members of any group of historically marginalized people in America (i.e., students of color, special needs, under-resourced, etc.). Therefore, teachers must realize and own their differentness. Even when they share the same race as their students, teachers often view school as a platform for ridding historically marginalized students of their differentness and encouraging them to check it at the door in order for teachers to emphasize mainstream values and behaviors.

In a professional learning meeting focused on motivating students, I once listened to a disgruntled teacher announce, "These kids don't care about ANYTHING! Nothing I do motivates them because they just don't care to learn!" My face and neck started to twitch, as I forced myself to suppress the HULK-like emotions rushing through my veins. Such an inflammatory statement by a teacher who openly expressed her disdain for our students over and over again pushed me to the edge of professional composure. This time she dared to say it in the presence of the team.

I raised my hand and waited patiently for my turn before reminding her, "I'm pretty sure they may not be motivated by the things that interest a 40-year-old, middle-class, White woman, but they are motivated by things that interest them." Later on, that teacher continued to have a hard time reaching students, and she eventually went to another school that I pray was a better match for her. Still, the truth is many teachers harbor similar feelings, though they may not vocalize such a belief. The term "these kids" clearly was the term she used to separate them from herself. That feeling of superiority that she held was rooted in her idea of the rightness of her whiteness. She couldn't fathom that the TV shows and songs she found worthy of classroom inclusion just didn't connect with her students.

The truth is all students come to us with a rich tapestry of knowledge and experiences. It is the responsibility of the paid-professional-educator in the room to become a student of students and to craft learning experiences that capitalize on students' strengths and validate the prior knowledge they possess.

Keep It 💯

The term *Keeping it 100* is an urban colloquialism that refers to one's ability to be completely transparent. Transparency of the teacher is essential. When it comes to teachers making learning relevant to students, teachers must be willing to open up. Not only does this openness help in relationship building, but it helps students see the genuine passion a teacher has (or should have) for the content they teach. As an English teacher, I encountered some students who abhorred writing. No matter how much I explained the cathartic power of writing, the bearing of my soul and experiences, was the difference between some of them buying in or not.

One major part of the lesson cycle in my classroom was the modeling piece or the "I Do." This was the part of the lesson where I went first by voyaging into the learning for the day and welcoming the kiddos to come along with me. Once during an English I lesson, the students were writing vignettes of detailed descriptions of a moment that changed their lives forever. Immediately, when they heard the objective, many students expressed their discontent and explained that they had not encountered anything they felt worthy of their writing. Then came my chance to go first, as the leader of our English odyssey! So, I scribbled a version of the following vignette from my childhood on the board, erasing, editing, and thinking aloud as I wrote, allowing students to observe the naturally recursive process of writing as I went along:

> The house felt like an icebox when they drove the sunshine away. Collapsing to my knees, I was a waste of useless tears. Useless because he didn't care. Useless because the police didn't care either. Useless because the tears of a 10-year-old don't prevent a domestic dispute. It was the day I saw my mother arrested and taken to jail.

Both arms folded behind her back. Escorted down the walkway to the back of a police car, per the demands of the tyrant she called "husband." I packed my bags, frantically, and ran as far as I could, as fast as I could. That was the day I knew I'd never trust a man the way she'd trusted him.

The class was frozen. Then naturally, students began hitting me with a barrage of questions:

"Did you make that up, Ms. B?"

"That didn't really happen, did it?"

One after the other, my students had a newfound interest in the vignette's objective. After that, their pens started pushing. The students were ready to write about their own experiences. The truth is I received a level of transparency I was not prepared for. Of all the vignettes I heard that week, I'll never forget the student who wrote about the day she got into a fistfight and experienced her first miscarriage. She opened with a line about how the warm blood streamed down her inner thighs. I can't make this stuff up: A sophomore girl. A miscarriage at the hands of a street fight.

This level of authenticity resulted from me keeping it 100 and giving students an environment for all of us to be safe to share. It was powerful. Transparency helps students to see our humanity as teachers. We aren't some porcelain props on permanent classroom display. Many of us have had to overcome challenges that may be similar to those our students are facing. Our willingness to open up gives students permission to do the same.

Get Plugged In

Whether you receive notifications from the latest news platforms, all day long, or still enjoy unrolling a fresh newspaper in the morning over coffee, one thing is sure: the information highway moves 1,000 miles per hour. This is the world we live in. As fast as events can happen, information becomes available to the world. Live video streams and 24-hour news cycles are the way of the world. If you want to have relevant instruction, you have to plug in. I don't mean to suggest that all teachers have to drive themselves crazy trying to keep up with receiving a million notifications to their cell phones (I hate those pesky things). Instead, teachers should plan to plug in.

There may be 1 day a week when lesson planning where a teacher searches the web for what's trending on Twitter. Teachers can do this without owning an account, just to see what's going on in the world and to think about how any of those things may connect to the standards that will be covered in the upcoming lesson. Even when serving young kids at the elementary level, you'd be surprised how much your students know when they hear grown-ups talking about current events.

The great news is that relevant activities and lessons are at a teacher's fingertips in this digital age! There are websites full of teachers sharing best practices and tools to use that specialize in relevance to students. The beauty of being plugged in is that once you have assessed your students' interests, you can use that information to find lessons, activities, and resources that catapult your assignments to the next level. Many educators view it as a daunting task to create innovative ideas. Still, there are enough online resources to help teachers create an arsenal of relevant lessons that students can connect to authentically.

In addition to plugging in with external sources that inform teaching practice, being plugged in internally is essential. As a teacher, I was a master eavesdropper. When students were in the hallways, I listened to what they were talking about, what songs they were singing, what terrible gossip was burning their tongues.

Side note: The key to being a master eavesdropper is to resist the urge to react to the outrageous things you hear and act like you don't hear the kids, so they continue to talk and not notice you listening.

Earlier in the chapter, I mentioned my use of a student informant when creating a bellringer. Student informants are another efficient way to stay plugged in internally. Every teacher has students with the potential to be their informants. They are the ones who come early and/or leave late. They are your helpers. They want to pass out and collect the papers for you. They want to speak to you in the hallway, and they are oftentimes just sweethearts. This may sound predatory, but it's not. Use them! Ask your informants follow-up questions about things you overheard in the hallway or the cafeteria. Ask them about what's going on with a student whom you've noticed a change of behavior with when the student won't open up. Ask your informant about the party that happened in the neighborhood the weekend before. Ask them what they thought about the lesson and activity in class that day or how you could have made it better.

Your informants will tell you what you want to know. They will be happy to be your informant, especially when they see lessons that reflect what's going on based on the information they have provided you. Never ever disclose who your informants are, as students will always ask questions like, "How did you know that, Miss? Who told you about that?" My standard answer was, "I'm all-knowing and ever-present, like God." 😂 😂 👻

Seeing is Believing

As an English IV Advanced Placement (AP) British Literature student, I had an incredible teacher, Mary Linnstaedter, who loved us greatly. However, I noticed halfway through learning about dozens of British authors that they all happened to be old, White men. There's nothing wrong with old, White men (just to be clear). I was just an inquisitive student unafraid to push the envelope (it's AP right?) so one day I politely asked, "Ms. Linn, did they have any Black people in Britain?" I mean, I'd never been there, so as far as I knew, there were no British writers that looked like me, and the content we read was far removed from my experience. My teacher, clearly unprepared for such a question, responded, "Oh, Stephanie!" as she squinted her eyes in my direction lovingly continuing on with the lesson.

Students need to see diversity in the subject and content you present. Let's take science, for instance. Consider the image of a scientist being some wiry-haired White man in a freshly pressed lab coat standing amidst mysterious vials of strange liquids he had concocted in the lab. If students are not otherwise exposed to diversity in various areas, they will believe what they see. Educators must go out of their way to diversify the images students see, so students understand the world is full of opportunities and possibilities. It's equally crucial for all students to see and understand the contributions of diverse groups to the progress of our country as a whole, as those contributions have been historically minimalized or left out altogether.

Suppose the only perceived images of success students see that look like them happen to come from professional athletes, entertainers, and God for-bid, the neighborhood drug dealer. In that case, their perceptions of success have to be reshaped in classrooms.

Let's take the idea of Bill Nye, the science guy's show, and Tyler the Creator's show Nuts + Bolts. You can check out the trailer here: https://www.youtube.com/watch?v=wwBCD-_Jt1o

This example is not to dismiss the value of Bill Nye at all (you see him featured in the video), but to help you understand the importance of a healthy balance in representation. Validation of the spectrum of contributors in every field, especially those where people of color are historically excluded, is a must in schools.

While working at a middle school with predominantly Black students, I can recall the principal, an African American mathematician herself, ordering a set of posters that highlighted African Americans of STEM that were col-or-coordinated according to the field of contribution: Science, Technology, Engineering, and Math. You can learn more about those here: https://www.itsablackthang.com/products/african-americans-of-stem-poster-set

Although I was an adult, I was elated to see the contributions highlighted in that poster set. Teachers in FRESH classrooms make this level of inclusion a regular experience for their students.

Give Students Choices! ⬚ ⬚ ⬚

The most challenging part of giving students choices is teachers relinquishing control. Yes, pause and breathe. In the FRESH Classroom Workshops with teachers, one question I get regularly is, "How do I make learning activities relevant to all students when all students are different?" Teachers are very concerned about the logistics of implementing what they learn about stu-dents into the classroom. My answer is simple: Give them choices!

With 1st grade students, that may mean choosing an activity or book centered around Doc McStuffins, Superman, or another character they are interested in (you need only refer to your students' backpack characters to assess their interests) and centered on their cultural diversity. It may mean allowing students to find a scene from their favorite school-appropriate movie to utilize for a plot analysis activity in high school. No matter how much variation you concoct, you can feel reassured that the more you give students the option to choose, the more receptive they will be when you do not give them a choice.

I know many educators have started to abhor the D word... Differentiation, but now is the appropriate time to discuss it. As a classroom teacher and instructional coach, I received quite a bit of professional development about differentiation. Half the training confused me more than it helped me, partially because I have a brain that constantly seeks to take complicated information and streamline it to something sensible. If you would like a deep dive into differentiation, let me recommend you refer to the work of Carol Ann Tomlinson. Here's a brief summation of her approach excerpted from her article titled "What is Differentiated Instruction?":

Teachers can differentiate at least four classroom elements based on student readiness, interest, or learning profile:

- **Content** – what the student needs to learn or how the student will get access to the information;

- **Process** – activities in which the student engages in order to make sense of or master the content;

- **Products** – culminating projects that ask the student to rehearse, apply, and extend what he or she has learned in a unit; and

- **Learning environment** – the way the classroom works and feels.

You can learn more from: https://www.readingrockets.org/article/what-differentiated-instruction

For brevity, I'd like to encourage teachers venturing into differentiation to focus on varying inputs and outputs. Inputs refer to the ways students take in new information. Some students may be auditory processors. Others may need visual aids to understand better, and kinesthetic learners may still benefit more by getting hands-on. While many educators may be inclined to teach in the way they learn best, FRESH educators push themselves to consider the diversity of the learning styles present in their classrooms.

For example, I am a visual learner. If a graph, flow chart, pictograph, etc., is comprehensive, I may not need a person to explain a new concept to me verbally at all. I see it clearly, and I get it. Visual input works for me. When it comes to output, I am more inclined to verbally explain what I've learned.

Output refers to how learners communicate what they know or understand. This output usually presents itself in a product that students turn into the teacher for a grade that should assess their mastery of the content. Differentiating output means allowing students to have a choice in how they illustrate the knowledge they gained from the lesson you covered in class.

One constructive approach I remember sharing with a group of teachers in a follow-up support session was learning menus. Learning menus give students options of which activities they want to complete over the course of a lesson, from the appetizer to the entree to the dessert. The Teaching Channel has a great example of this menu at https://learn.teachingchannel.com/video/differentiating-instruction-strategy

No matter how you go about creating choices for your students, just know this perception of choice (I mean, you still generated the options) will provide students a different level of autonomy in the learning process. Their self-selection will also help you better understand which types of activities they prefer as you continue learning about and implementing more of the things they know. That's FRESH.

Plan with a Team

The days of the island teacher are gone. Teamwork definitely makes the dream work in schools. Keeping up with evolving technology trends, educational innovation, and state and federal mandates requires a pooling of brainpower. In the upcoming section of Culturally Proficient Learning Communities, I detail the research that spells out the importance of teachers working together in their efforts to implement culturally relevant lessons with fidelity.

These days, most schools already have some commitment to ensuring teachers receive time to plan together. While they take on many different names: professional learning communities (PLC), team planning period, cluster meeting, etc., the purpose is to provide teachers with some time to collaborate around sharing best practices and mapping out weekly lessons. Everyone has different ideas about how these meetings should unfold and what they should focus on primarily. I've observed PLCs with teams that start each session with data from formative assessments students have taken the previous week, then moved into action plans for interventions in the upcoming week. I've also observed PLCs where team members decompress and complain about their unruly students until they run down the clock for the meeting time.

The truth is educators have to maximize their time if they are going to keep their classrooms FRESH. Here are some tips for keeping your planning time FRESH:

1. **Data/Student Work:** Plan to bring in data from the assessments and/or student work samples from the week before. Take time to share and compare student outcomes as a team. Be sure that student work samples are not all high mastery examples. Agree as a team to bring in high, medium, and low work according to your grading standard. This practice allows the team to anchor the meeting in what matters, student outcomes.

2. **Map the Week**: Using your district's curriculum guide, identify what standards will be covered each day of the week. This is a great time to determine what prerequisite skills are necessary for mastery of the weekly standards. It will be required to know these when scaffolding (more info to come on scaffolding in upcoming chapters).

3. **Identify Resources**: Determine what resources you will use in the daily lesson activities (i.e., textbooks, online websites, exciting videos, helpful handouts, etc.). This is the step where we can dig

into connecting with students. Get plugged in and see how you can make this relevant to your students. Know what's going on in the school community this week, what current events have the students buzzing, and what important community figures could be utilized.

If these basics can be covered in a planning session, the other particulars of the lesson may vary from teacher to teacher. Some teams prefer to work in lockstep with their bellringers, station activity, and assessments being identical. Other groups value having a little more autonomy over the nuts and bolts of the lesson. I think that each campus's decision must be made internally, so I won't project my preference. All I'll say is don't reinvent the wheel if you don't have to. Teaching is a hard job, so the more time we can save, the better.

Kill the Paper Lesson Plan

When it comes to team planning, I also can't let this section pass without admonishing readers to strongly consider killing the paper lesson plan. If you haven't already seen my YouTube video on this topic, do yourself a favor and check it out at: https://www.youtube.com/watch?v=6fFRmm7zl5w . Essentially, I encourage educational leaders to move into the 21st century by permitting educators to submit their slide decks that facilitate the daily lessons. As a principal, I didn't have my teachers upload paper lesson plans via Microsoft Word documents with rows and columns filled with the lesson segments. Instead, each teacher created a slide deck for that week, and each step of the lesson was laid out, as the students would see it. In the notes section of each slide, the teacher would detail any information that wasn't for students to see (i.e., grouping info for stations, backup links to embedded videos, general notes to self).

Since my teachers were using Google Slides, we were all seeing and editing the document in real-time when we sat down for their lesson plan reviews. This was a more collaborative approach that saved us all time. Traditionally, teachers submit a file, wait on feedback, update the file, then, based on what is on the lesson plan document, build an actual slide deck to guide students through the lesson stages. By cutting to the last step, I was able to see every standard-aligned objective, embedded video, engaging picture, and every link to an online game platform. By the end of our lesson plan reviews, the daily lessons were both instructionally sound and aesthetically intriguing for students. *Side note: These slides were also convenient if a student missed class and needed to make up the lesson and activities they missed that day.

When teachers plan together using these slide decks, they can update and shoot feedback to each other throughout the day about what's working best and what's not. The lesson's relevance increases when teachers streamline this information in real-time and not just drag on with ineffective lessons over the course of a day, until they make it to their next planning session to discuss what worked and what did not. Just try it out, and if it doesn't work, you can blame it on this book and go back to the traditional approach. No harm, no foul. 👻

Home Languages Matter

Home languages refer to the languages and dialects students learn and use outside of school. While most people think about home languages strictly in terms of bilingual students, educators must understand the different ways people can speak aside from Standard English (SE). Many people have grown accustomed to referring to various linguistic iterations as "broken English," but I don't believe there's anything broken about variation. This idea is a challenge to the Euro-centered norms we have been taught as necessary to communicate brilliance. As educators, we can teach students to use SE and respect the varieties of that language they already possess and utilize outside of schools.

For example, I grew up in Dallas, Texas, and surrounding areas where African American Vernacular English (AAVE) was used fluently. However, I came to understand how AAVE varies on a spectrum based on geographical location on my first trip to New Orleans, Louisiana as a young girl. While we were visiting people who looked like us, I was immediately jarred by how differently their Creole accents sounded to my Dallas-native ears. Were they speaking English? Primarily - you know, they slide a little French in frequently. But the thick dialect and cadence of their speech definitely left me doing more listening than talking, as I learned to understand this new flavor my ears were experiencing for the first time.

After visiting New Orleans for years, I now know exactly what it means to "make groceries" or get a "cold cup," terms that definitely confused me on that first trip. 😎 If I'm in New Orleans and find myself amongst natives, I may even start to drift into using the dialect myself (a shameful imitation at best). But this total cultural emersion I experienced, at an early age, (especially during Mardi Gras seasons) helped me better understand the people in New Orleans and appreciate their culture and differences.

The truth is many students of color that have mastered their home languages have to learn to code-switch when they come into academic settings. Code-switching is defined as the combining of two or more languages or dialects. To be accepted into some spaces, many people of color learn early that their home languages will be judged as wrong, especially by educators unfamiliar with their variations of English. This judgment, both verbal and non-verbal, is internalized by students and can foster feelings of shame. Teachers must be careful not to frown upon and degrade students' home languages.

Instead, teachers must help students navigate contexts and determine when it is appropriate to use their home languages vs. Standard English. Perhaps when they are in class, the teacher will expect them to speak and write in SE, a skill I am not diminishing. But when they are in the cafeteria or hallways connecting with friends, policing of home languages can start to feel like educational colonization.

In her brilliant TED Talk "3 Ways to Speak English," Jamila Lyiscott hails herself as a "trilingual orator," wielding the ability to switch up her oral delivery whether she's at home, school, or with friends. This skill becomes a superpower for those who have to navigate academic, social, political, and professional settings without being linguistically profiled and erroneously labeled as unintelligent. FRESH teachers don't just seek to better students' home languages; they celebrate and invite them into the school community.

FRESH Lesson Planning Questions:

1. Why should students care about this standard/skill?
2. Are the resources provided in my textbook sufficient to engage my students?
3. Where do they see it in the real world?
4. How can I include that real-world application in this lesson?
5. What's trending this week?
6. How did my students rate the relevance of last week's learning activities?

Chapter 8

E = Engaging

Student engagement with content is one of the most critical aspects of lessons that create transferable knowledge. According to Edgar Dale (1969), 2 weeks after a learning experience, we remember 10% of what we read, 20% of what we hear, and 30% of what we see! Now, when we can hear, see, and do, our ability to retain new information increases to 90% during a learning experience. But didn't we already know that? I think we did. When it comes to engagement, the biggest issue I see in schools has less to do with what we know and more to do with what we execute in daily instruction. When it comes to engagement, let's be clear that there are ways to get students leaning in and engaging with the content, no matter the subject area. We just have to be willing to get out of our comfort zones and into the FRESH zone!

How Do I Make My Teaching Engaging?

Engagement comes in different forms; however, I often hear the term used when teachers refer to student-to-student engagement (i.e., small group and cooperative learning activities). While this is one way to engage students, I will also address two other engagement points: student-to-teacher engagement and student-to-community engagement.

Student-to-Student Engagement

In FRESH classrooms, lessons intentionally allow students to interact with each other to reach a specific learning goal. Early on, I discovered that elementary educators were more likely to use small group and station activities to get students engaged with different activities. In contrast, in secondary classrooms, students were made to sit, listen, then work the majority of the instructional time independently. It is almost as if students no longer needed as much engagement, and they should be able to shut up and soak up information for hours a day. It's no wonder we see many students lose their zest for learning as they move into upper grades.

Problem-Based Group Tasks

When I started implementing small groups at the high school level, I was surprised to see how my students responded. Once we took time to be sure each student in the group had a role and knew the responsibility attached to that role, students could work together and rock and roll. While some teachers may define an effective learning environment as a quiet, rule-regulated, controlled space where the teacher is centered, I outright rejected that notion. My instructional goal was to facilitate the learning and let students work together through the learning experiences.

Student-to-student engagement is less about students checking off boxes in a series of activities together and more about the authentic exchange of ideas and collective striving.

Many students are social beings, and having the opportunity to work together through the learning allows them to use that urge for socializing with each other for a pointed objective that you have provided them for the day. Although we cannot have students spend every minute of every lesson engaged with one another, a FRESH class allows students to engage with each other throughout the lesson in targeted and specific ways.

Peer-Led Lessons

The cultural capital students possess is extensive and typically more aligned to other students than anything the teacher can understand. For this reason, I encourage educators to turn over the reins of teaching new content and let the students take the lead. This approach happens to be more effective when there are clear boundaries and expectations set in advance for students, and the teacher has vetted what they will teach before they teach it. I mean, I believe in my students, but I ain't a fool. When a student was in charge of the lesson for the day, I was sure that I had reviewed their presentation in advance and provided feedback accordingly.

Student-to-Teacher Engagement

To many people, the whole-group, direct teaching approach that comes from the teacher standing at the front of the room would be considered student-to-teacher engagement. Still, I argue that lecturing students from a distance is only one way (and the least impactful, depending on the compelling power of the lecture) that the teacher may engage with students. Don't get me wrong, I've heard some talks that engaged 99% of the students in the room and had them on the edge of their seats, but even the most riveting lecture can only hold the attention of adolescents for so long (or even my interest as an adult for that matter). Because I understand the power that a good lecture can have, I have to acknowledge it as a form of student-to-teacher engagement.

That being said, FRESH teachers keep a toolbox full of tricks to engage their students. Small group activities are one such tool. While the grouping size and arrangement may vary based on the class size and objective of the lesson activities, these kinds of activities are characteristic of FRESH lessons. As young as pre-kindergarten and as old as 12th grade, I have seen teachers facilitate small groups in a way that gets them authentically engaged with students.

One such configuration I've observed is when teachers set up at one station to deliver new content or review previously taught material; at the other small groups, students have been instructed on what they will do, and written instructions are left for them to refer to. After getting all the other small groups started, the teacher is stationed with one group. After an allotted amount of time, the groups rotate, and the next group of students receives small group instruction from the teacher. This rotation continues as many times as the teacher deems necessary to complete the instructional goals for each group.

Student-to-Community Engagement

While we typically focus on engagement in the context of students and teachers and activities in the classroom, FRESH teachers understand that authentic engagement must extend outside of the four walls of school buildings. If educators want learning to be transferrable for the students we teach, we must engage them with our content in the real world.

As a principal, I made it my business to ensure we had about three field trips a month on the schedule. While these trips were not inclusive of every student, every time, there were options based on the content being covered and extracurricular involvement. When planning a unit, teachers were required to locate a place they could take students or get guests into the school in a meaningful way connected to the learning in that unit.

For example, in a science class, to make the real-world connection to the community around them, students had to learn about the ecosystem surrounding the school as they started a classroom garden from beginning to end. At the project's onset, students went to the Dallas Arboretum to see the fabulous gardens and flowers. In the end, a representative from the Arboretum came to our campus to give the students feedback on their class garden. These are what I call full-circle learning moments. I will explain more details of this and other projects in the H = Higher Order section of this book.

While educators often get focused on planning within the context of classrooms, FRESH teachers identify valuable resources and community partners that can bring a much-needed dynamic to the work we do in schools. Many companies, governmental entities, and organizations are often looking for ways to get more involved in their communities. Planning FRESH lessons means taking the time to think outside the box regarding when and where these skills or concepts will be used/seen in the world around us. The more students see the skills and concepts they encounter in the real-world context, the more critical our content becomes.

While many educators understand the concept of field trips as necessary, many schools reduce their value to an ancillary status and save them for end-of-the-year treats for their students who have behaved throughout the school year and done well on state assessments. The FRESH classroom is all about making these experiences regular occurrences (it's not always as pricey as it sounds if it's done correctly and planned in advance).

Here are some ways to make field trips and campus guests a regular part of what you do.

1. **Map out your units.** Most teachers receive a scope and sequence that outlines what they will cover throughout the school year and when. For many teachers, that pacing stays the same for years at a time, so once a team has done the work of discovering some community connections, they should be able to maintain them for years to come. Ask yourself where are the skills and knowledge you will be teaching in that unit seen and utilized in the community. For example, if you teach students about the life cycle and there's a local veterinarian's office or zoo, contact them to share what your students will be learning and then ask for their support as far in advance as you can.

2. **Solicit support.** Create a form letter, or borrow the one I created in the "Guide to Building Authentic Community Connections" at www.thefreshclassroom.com/freebies. Disseminate letters to potential community partners, and if at all possible, plan to make those contacts over the summer or early fall. You will be so surprised by how many community partners love to be invited into schools to understand how they can support kids. They simply need an invitation to come in and clear-cut directives concerning how they may be of value. This type of support should not be limited to career day. All year long, the content and skills children are learning are related to the real world, so let's show them how. Start early and think big!

FRESH Lesson Planning Questions:

1. Have I included all three types of engagement in my lessons for the upcoming week?
2. When will students get to DO the learning in the lessons I am preparing?
3. Are my students moving from the passive ways of learning (i.e., read, hear, see) to active forms of learning (i.e., saying and doing)?
4. What roles have I created for student-to-student engagement that will keep students on-task and productive?

Chapter 9

S = Standards-Based

At this point in my teacher training, I am always sure to emphasize that teachers should never get caught up in trying to make things so relevant and fun they forget about the standards. I make sure they understand they WILL get fired (those words literally appear in the slide). And while we all laugh at that, the weight of mandated standards and assessments means teachers have to be very clear about balancing the art of teaching (fun, relevant, engaging) with the science of education (standards-based and higher-order).

When they lack content knowledge, many teachers over-rely on textbooks and curricular guides created by people who have never met their students. Instead of these resources being employed at the teacher's instructional discretion, they become like crutches. This is what I often encounter as the downfall of the rookie teacher. As a new teacher, it's tempting to go too far to one extreme or the other and come up short. But in all things, the goal must be alignment. In my second year of teaching, someone explained it to me using a graphic similar to the one adapted for you seen below. As a visual learner, this graphic helped me better grasp the connection between the what (curriculum), the how (instruction), and the measurement (assessment) of what educators do.

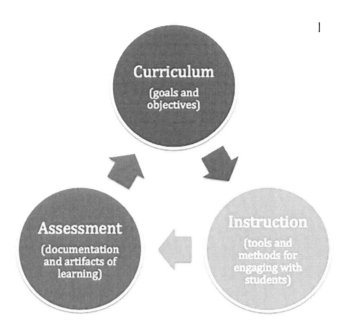

While we could spend time exploring the negative aspects of standardized testing and culture-neutral curricula in schools, this book is focused on helping you as educators improve your practice within the current contexts that exist in your schools. There are, without doubt, opportunities for curriculum to be more inclusive of the total American experience and more robust ways to assess students than multiple choice scantrons, but truth be told, many educators are seeing success with students despite the laundry list of things they'd love to change about the system. You can be one of them!

HOW DO I ENSURE MY TEACHING IS STANDARDS-BASED?

The most obvious first step here is to become a content area expert. This is the reason I am always such an advocate for departmentalization in elementary classrooms (clearly, I started in secondary, so ... yeah). While some exams leading to teaching certifications may require mastery of some things, a certified teacher can exist without having a deep understanding of the standards they are certified to teach. Sounds crazy, right? Hi, my name is Stephanie Boyce (formerly Ms. Barton), and I am Exhibit A.

After graduating with a bachelor's degree in Psychology, I studied and passed the necessary exams to gain certification to teach English Language Arts for Grades 8 through 12. While my alternative certification program taught me how to make a lesson plan and some essentials like managing classroom behavior, I never got a deep dive into my content until I was teaching it. Yep, good ole on-the-job training. Under the right set of circumstances (i.e., on-campus mentoring, team lesson planning, ongoing professional development, etc.), I managed to learn and teach and not ruin the lives of those seniors (shout out to Thurgood Marshall High School class of 2010). Yet, I was also in an English department that boasted of its 90% and higher passing rates on state assessments and moved in lockstep with lesson plans. This level of support held me up where my content knowledge was short, and my passion was long.

Meaningful, Engaging, Hands-On Content Training

When consulting with educational leaders looking to book The FRESH Classroom Workshop, I always ask them if their teachers have already received good training for their content areas, as our time together will dive into their pedagogical approaches and not into the content they teach. It's always my belief that stellar content training is the cornerstone of a teachers' approach. If teachers don't have a strong command of what to teach, the "how" to teach conversation is irrelevant.

As an assistant principal, I had the pleasure to intern under one of the best principals with whom I have ever been blessed to work, Dr. Tonya Howard. At her lead, teachers, instructional coaches, and assistant principals took an entire released state assessment that students in their grade level would be required to take annually. As a principal, I also required my teachers to do the same thing. These assessments (even the 3rd-grade ones) were freaking hard! I have seen grown, degreed, and fully certified educators fail the exact tests their students had to take in years past. Think I'm lying? When's the last time you took one? Having educators get hands-on with these assessments was one way to cultivate empathy and understanding for students, help them analyze the test-taking strategies they employ instinctively and need to convey to students, and prepare them to create classroom assessments that could match the rigor of the state standards. Starting the year with this hands-on activity was great data going into professional development for content expertise.

Teachers need deep, meaningful, and practical professional development to help them unpack wordy standards and get to the meat of what students are supposed to be able to DO. The best example of this kind of professional development I've ever experienced was the "Laying the Foundations" training. In this training, teachers spent countless hours over a week going lesson by lesson, completing assignments and activities, as if we were the students. By the end of the week, the booklets they had given us were marked up, highlighted, and annotated to death. We had engaged and enjoyed ourselves in the process, and we were mentally exhausted (Happy Hour me, please). These professional development experiences put teachers in the role of students and allow them to understand what students need to DO to master the content standards.

Break It, Break It Down!

Let's dive deeper into the DO. I keep capitalizing DO because DOing so much more critical than the hear or see (we've already covered that in the Engagement section). So, let's look at a standard, and drill down. In Texas, the Texas Essential Knowledge and Skills (TEKS) are the state standards that tell us what students should know and DO in each class. Many helpful online tools exist to help educators analyze and better understand their standards. One such tool that I found helpful is Lead Forward (https://lead4ward.com/). Their expansive bank of resources spans from data tools to instructional tools. Because I started teaching high school and it's in my heart, let's begin with an English I standard:

> E1.7E: Analyze characteristics and structural elements of argumentative texts such as:
>
> E1.7E.i: clear, arguable claim, appeals, and convincing conclusion;
>
> E1.7E.ii: various types of evidence and treatment of counterarguments, including concessions and rebuttals; and

E1.7E.iii: identifiable audience or reader.

For the sake of this illustration, I will focus on the highlighted portion of the standard (E.1.7E.ii). When analyzing standards, I encourage teachers to ask the following questions:

- What is the standard requiring students to do (Focus on the verbs)?
- What is the subject/focus of the standard?
- What would students need to know already?

After reading the highlighted portion, I know that students would need to understand what counterarguments, including concessions and rebuttals, are when they see them in a text. Now, as I begin to brainstorm which argumentative texts to use for the lesson, I allow my mind to float to R = Relevant as I start to brainstorm various argumentative texts on a variety of topics based on the interest of my students. In the FRESH Classroom, we always start with the standard, then build a bridge to the relevance for students. It's a simple formula that can go far when we do it with fidelity.

As a field supervisor for the college of education at a university, I was charged with coaching teachers who were education majors engaging in their student-teaching internships in schools. One thing that I quickly realized was a challenge for some of them and other educators I've mentored, for that matter, was having the ability to create learning experiences that required students to get to the depth of the verb. Let's use our example from the highlighted standard previously listed.

Analyze characteristics and structural elements of argumentative texts such as:

E1.7E. ii: various types of evidence and treatment of counterarguments, including concessions and rebuttals.

What's the verb listed in the standard, or the thing students must DO for any instructional activity to be aligned to this standard? Yes, it's "*analyze*." Now, one of the main topics of my coaching came when I saw teachers' instructional activities require students to do the much simpler action of "identifying" instead of "analyzing." Let's look at an example using an excerpt from one of the most skilled debaters I have ever studied, El-Hajj Malik El-Shabazz, more widely known as and referred to, hereafter, as Malcolm X.

Due to the revolutionary nature of his approach and ideology, he had to become a master of weaving in concessions and rebuttals in his efforts to both refute his former emphasis on converting Black people to the Nation of Islam, frequently offending Black Christians with his scathing critiques, and moving toward a more unifying message of Black Nationalism. Consider this excerpt from his 1964 speech entitled "The Bullet or the Ballot":

> The economic philosophy of Black Nationalism only means that we should own, and operate, and control the economy of our community. You can't open up a Black store in a White community. White men won't even patronize you. And he's not wrong! He's got sense enough to look out for himself. It's you who don't have sense enough to look out for yourself...
>
> So, our people not only have to be re-educated to the importance of supporting Black business, but the Black man himself has to be made aware of the importance of going into business. And once you and I go into business, we own and operate at least the businesses in our community. What we will be doing is developing a situation, wherein, we will actually be able to create employment for the people in the community. And once you can create some employment in the community where you live, it will eliminate the necessity of you and me having to act ignorantly and disgracefully, boycotting and picketing some c----- someplace else trying to beg him for a job...
>
> Whether you are a Christian or a Muslim or a nationalist, we all have the same problem. They don't hang you because you're a Baptist; they hang you because you're Black. They don't attack me because I'm a Muslim. They attack me because I'm Black. They attacked all of us for the same reason. All of us catch hell from the same enemy. We're all in the same bag, in the same boat.

Quoted accessed at:

https://www.rev.com/blog/transcripts/
the-ballot-or-the-bullet-speech-transcript-malcolm-x

If you are unfamiliar with the rhetoric of Malcolm X and feel a little triggered after reading, take a second to breathe and digest this excerpt. Come back to the book when you're ready to move forward, analyzing the elements of the argumentative text, separate from your particular ideas about Malcolm X's position.

Now, let's get back to our activity. One of the biggest causes for concern with many educators is that they think students cannot move to the higher-level verbs (like analyze) if they are coming into class already below grade level not yet mastering the lower-level verbs (like identify). Therefore, teachers may design a lesson activity that causes students to spend the entirety of the class learning to identify types of evidence and counterarguments and never get to the analysis level. This is a big mistake that keeps students behind the eight ball. Instead, teachers have to assess where students are intellectually and scaffold lessons accordingly while modeling what success looks like.

Scaffolding

Scaffolding, in this context, refers to breaking the learning activities into chunks that allow students to move along the scale from a lower-level to a higher-level skill throughout a given amount of instructional time. Let's use our standard from above. Suppose my pre-assessment before this day's lesson revealed that about half of my students have difficulty identifying types of evidence and/or counterarguments in argumentative texts.

In that case, I may start half of the students out on an activity where they and a group of their peers (grouped homogeneously according to their ability) worked first to define different types of evidence frequently used in argumentative texts and types of counterarguments (i.e., concessions and rebuttals). They may do something simple like a matching or pairing activity that helps them quickly make those primary connections, but students would not spend the bulk of their time at this step, or they will inevitably run out of time. They would quickly move from getting a grasp on that concept to seeing examples based on snippets of another text where they now see these examples applied to an actual text. Next, the group may identify a couple of examples in the main text from the day's lesson (the Malcolm X piece). Then, using some sentence stems that assist with analyzing texts, they may go on to doing some analyses on their own.

Modeling

Another very particular way to break down what is expected of students, in any standard, is for the teacher to provide some extensive modeling of the expectations. As an ELAR teacher, I can't tell you how many times I used an overhead projector (yes, I'm an OG) or a projected slide deck or word document to model writing expectations in real-time for students (refer to the example I shared in the section about making lessons Relevant).

During my Top Model segments of the lesson, my standard rule was "when I write, you write." This rule prohibited students from staring on idly, as I slaved away at the board or computer for them to just forget what I said 5 minutes later, forsaking all my hard work and brainpower. Instead, they turned to a new section of their interactive notebooks (yes, I was one of those teachers) and wrote down any examples I'd provided for their future reference. Many otherwise stuck students would be able to take off on their own after simply seeing my example. In order for modeling to be effective, consider doing the following:

- **Be consistent**. Model when you're introducing a new skill or concept no matter how long or brief your example may be. Let students know that it isn't for them to copy in their responses, but to see what success looks like.

- **Think aloud**. As you model, say your thoughts out loud for students to hear, flaws and all. I would let students see me say one word, then scratch it out and use a more precise term. Modeling isn't about perfection; it's about process.

- **Be thorough**. While some examples are already prepared for students to see, modeling happens in real-time, so that students are observing how you get from point A to point Z of the process. Don't ask them to join in like a "we do." This is time for your thoughts to become crystal clear. Even students who are "advanced" can sometimes benefit from hearing how your ideas unfold.

After you're sure about what the verb is requiring students to DO, you've considered the subject/focus of the standard, and you've thought through what they would need to know and scaffolded to that point and modeled your expectation, you will have successfully broken it down!

Authentic Assessments

While the backlash against standardized testing has been a constant reality in education for decades, in the post-COVID era of education, that backlash has reached a crescendo. I always stand with educators in voicing the disparities perpetuated by a singular focus on testing. For that reason, I always encourage educators to get involved in advocacy efforts (at the local, state, and national level) to call for changes in how our students are assessed and resourced. The research is clear concerning the deleterious effects of culturally biased, state-imposed tools used to disenfranchise students of color further.

Have I been clear enough about how I feel about these assessments? Good, because in the meantime, we all have to deal with the realities of the day, despite our theoretical objections and feelings. If there is a revolutionary approach to education, I think our classrooms are the perfect places to implement authentic assessments that align to standards and create a barrier of sanity for students while assessing what they can DO. Here are some of the examples I have either used as a classroom teacher or instructional leader:

- **Portfolios**: These represent a collection of a student's work designed to give a complete picture of a student's progress over a specified period of time.

- **Performances and exhibitions**: These may include speeches, science experiments, debates, artistic performances, mock trials, or publications.

- **Projects**: These allow students to investigate a subject of interest to them.

- **Learning logs and journals**: These are brief, factual entries that can include mathematical problem solving, science experiment observations, questions about lectures or readings, and connections to what is being learned in class.

- **Observation checklists**: Teachers, small groups, and individual students can use these to monitor specific skills or behaviors in students. They may include student's names, space for four or five targeted areas, a code or rating to determine demonstration of the skill, and space for comments.

- **Graphic organizers**: Venn diagrams, webs, and concept maps can be used to monitor students' thinking in the early stages of an assignment or unit.

- **Interviews and conferences**: Direct personal communication with students can elicit students' thoughts, opinions, and feelings about their work.

Problem/Project Based Learning

This is the part of the book where I make a hard-core appeal for project/ problem-based learning (PBLs). I know no better pivot into the rant I'm about to go on. During my time in education, I have not found a more authentically connected approach to teaching and learning than PBLs. By now, this approach is a lot more accepted in schools, but that trend was relatively new years ago when I was working in a district that committed to STEM education, and PBLs were a considerable part of that initiative. Let me add that much of the work we did was rooted in the resources provided by PBL Works (https://www.pblworks.org/). In addition to receiving a boatload of money for implementing these efforts, the district selected teams of PBL Pioneer Teachers, putting yours truly on the front lines of those efforts.

It was frustrating going from traditional, teacher-led, teacher-centered instruction to some pie-in-the-sky projects where students would lead the way. It was tough as hell for some teachers. It was a mindset shift, to say the least. I, low key, remember we did a book study using Carol Dweck's book *Mindset* ahead of the PBL training for this reason. Working with a team committed to figuring it out and doing the work was an enriching experience. Not only were PBLs centering students in the instructional experience, but they were also inherently culturally responsive to the students and community we served.

Take a second to look over the PBL timeline document below that provides abbreviated descriptions of what we covered in one of our early PBLs.

PBL Timeline At-A-Glance
9th/English

Problem or Question?	How do we use art forms to inspire the entrepreneurial spirit in minority communities? What have assimilation and integration done to cultural pride? How do people decide where they want to live? How do societies "corral" people into certain locations? How do societal norms influence perceptions of a community? How do limited resources affect the economic stability of a community?
Duration	11 Days
Summary	A minority developer wants to bring a shopping mall to Lancaster. However, he has reservations about the reputation and economic state of the community. He would like to know that the minority entrepreneurs in the city will invest in becoming a part of his development and to see evidence that Lancaster is more than the negative stigma placed upon it.
Focus SE (s)	1AB, D, F19A&B, 5B, 12A&D, 13A&E, 14B&C, 25A, 26A

Dates	Activities/Products/Formative Assessments
Day 1	LAUNCH-Movie Clip Entry Document , Know/Need to Know, Team Contracts Assign roles, preliminary research, logo, complete mission & vision statement
Day 2	Workshop – criteria chart for expository writing Research statistics and facts about the city of Lancaster and surrounding area Begin compiling report of findings
Day 3	Workshop – Types of poetry Discuss types of poetry to incorporate into presentation Begin writing poetry
Day 4	Continue working on reports and writing poetry
Day 5	Workshop – Elements of dramatic interpretations/presentations Youtube clips from A Different World and other Mammy presentation
Day 6	Workshop – Drama analysis Complete poems Completed reports due
Day 7	Workshop – Presentation etiquette Write scripts
Day 8	Practice presentations, Critical friends, Poems & Scripts
Day 9	Presentation Day
Day 10	Presentation Day
Day 11	Self and Peer Assessment, Debrief and celebration

If you pay attention to the summary of the PBL, you'll see we took an actual challenge to this under-resourced community (as is the case in many similar communities) where our students watch and can articulate the economic growth and opportunities seen in other towns that fail to show up in their community. They find that dollar stores are the fastest-growing businesses in their communities, only matched by fried chicken joints. It is with this understanding of the economic disparities facing their community that this project is rooted. However, this was still an ELAR I classroom (a state-tested subject), so rest assured the standards listed in the timeline anchored the daily assignments and were being continuously assessed.

FRESH educators understand it is the ultimate objective for culturally responsive classrooms to explore and discuss the disparities that exist in communities of color and, more importantly, cultivate critical thinking. FRESH educators are change agents, equipped with the brainpower to understand how to advocate and conspire for change.

Perhaps my favorite part of any of the PBLs I led or observed over the years was the presentation days. After students had worked hard on a project, we would always bring in authentic audience members (including community members and parents) to observe the student presentations. The audience could include a panel of participants from the fields represented in the project (i.e., business owners, commercial real estate investors, etc.) to judge the presentations and give students honest, rubric-based feedback on the effectiveness of the project products. This was the most authentic form of assessment. Once students realized outside people were going to actually evaluate their projects, their efforts increased. They wanted to polish their presentation slides, dress nicely, rehearse their parts in advance. I promise you, the amount of effort increased, as the authenticity did.

Let me lean in a little bit on the importance of students, as early as kindergarten, learning the essentials of effective presentations and having class time to hone presentation skills over the years. One of the most disheartening aspects of teaching high school seniors was observing students who had not been taught and trained in the essentials of oral presentation, despite preparing to graduate and go into the real world. It's like no one is testing students on their ability to speak publicly, and so many educators have low, if any, expectations. This is a tragic mistake. Not too many other skills will be as crucial to a student in the real world as the power to take a position on a topic; gather data, information, or evidence; organize their thoughts; and articulate their beliefs both in written and oral mediums. FRESH Classrooms must be spaces where students are regularly given the floor to speak, defend their positions, and know that their voices are valued. This is especially true of students in historically marginalized communities where schools have often minimized and silenced them.

How often do students invest time in a classroom assignment or project, only for the teacher to throw it away or scribble a grade on it and hand it back, never to be seen again? Our student's PBLs were more than any scantron could have ever measured. We saw them stand and deliver, speak facts to professionals, and research and employ innovative tech tools for presenting. (PowerPoints were outlawed by this time in the year to encourage mastery of various types of presentation tools.) These student-centered, community-focused projects became non-negotiable for me as a leader. However, by then, I'd come to understand the importance of taking the community connection to the next level. I'll tell you more about what that looked like in the FRESH section addressing the H = Higher-Order.

No Magic School Bus

(Because no teacher wants "that kid" in public)

I told you earlier that, right before 6th grade, my mother and I got a divorce from her husband. Divorce has serious implications for all kids, but divorce meant going back to lean times in my life. When my mother was married, two things happened: (1) we lived in a nice suburban neighborhood that actually had White people in it (I always assessed our economic status by the abundance of green yards and number of White people living in a particular area) and (2) I felt legitimized, in some way, when we were all out in public as a family. So, divorce meant no more green yards or White people in my neighborhood. It meant downsizing and eating cereal more often. It meant staying in apartment complexes. It meant Mom working more and having no vacations at the friendly time-share resort, but it also meant peace and having my mommy all to myself.

I hated the concrete slabs that replaced the freshly cut green lawns. I hated that my little brothers would be residing with their dad and not with my mom and me until weekends. That was a challenging year. My mom worked multiple jobs, sometimes, to make ends meet, and when school let out, I had to walk home from the intermediate school with all the other latchkey kids.

On the first day of school, I was mad and determined to hate the place, but I met a friend who would become my best friend for years to come: Jessica. Jessica was my saving grace. In addition to giving me the scoop on all of our classmates, she even made sure I had a walking partner after school. I'm still grateful for Jessica, to this day, for making it impossible for me to hate my new school forever. However, all the friendship in the world didn't take away from the fact that I was mad. Angry. Hurt. I was transitioning into a new normal and missing my little brothers and old friends.

One thing I vividly remember about the 6th grade is missing field trips. Because of the referrals I received during the year, I could not attend field trips. If there's one thing I know about teachers, it's that they absolutely abhor the idea of being embarrassed by a misbehaving student who goes off the rails in public. So, let's think about this.

Not only do students get punished for their behavior when the behavior occurs, but again, at the end of the year, when they miss out on yet another learning opportunity. Since my experience never leaves me, I often question my intentions and the intentions of other educators. Am I denying this child a learning opportunity because I don't believe the punishment they already received was sufficient? Or am I more concerned with the potential embarrassment of a misbehaving kid than I am about exposing that kid to a new world of learning? In my experience, the kids who presented the most extensive behavioral challenges were often the students who needed exposure to the world the most. So, as an administrator, I pushed teachers to take those challenging students (sometimes with a supervising guardian) to experience things they would otherwise never see.

I am fully aware that some extreme cases exist, but I believe we can extend grace more often to students who have a tough time instead of heaping double and triple punishments on them for their indiscretions. As a teacher and principal, I took students to see plays (I'll share more in the next section). I still remember taking two of my most behaviorally challenged students to see "A Christmas Carole" at the Dallas Theatre Center. Those matinee showings were held only for students, and I was determined to give those two their first trip to the theatre and NOT be embarrassed in the process.

For that reason, I made sure those two sat on either side of me in the theater (close enough for me to grab them, in a worst-case scenario, LOL). Clearly, their behavior issues had forfeited them the privilege of sitting with their friends, even though I had allowed them to come (I'm not crazy!). I also had to have a "come-to-Jesus" meeting with them and their parents before the trip to ensure they understood the consequences of any foolish behaviors. Those two, like all the other students I ever took on field trips, behaved wonderfully. It was like the stakes were high (right along with their engagement), and they rose to the occasion.

My experience being left out of school field trips gave me a perspective that always forced me to challenge myself. Before you let the Magic School Bus drive away and leave a child behind, ask yourself, have I exhausted every possible option to provide this kid with the learning experience for the day. After all, it is the learning experience for the day, not a relaxing beach vacation they should have to "earn" the right to enjoy. Think about it!

Chapter 10

H = Higher Order

"In the spirit of colonization, many schools stand in cultural opposition to the communities that surround them. Consequently, those communities come to deeply distrust the very educational institutions they send their kids to daily."
~ Dr. Stephanie Boyce
(Yes, I quoted myself. The book is almost over!)

When you mention the term higher-order, many educator's minds go straight to Bloom's Taxonomy, where the graphic image of the multi-colored triangle instantaneously emerges for their reference with descriptors that explain the ascending categories: remembering, understanding, applying, analyzing, evaluating, and creating.

This image represents one of the most widely referenced and accepted concepts in education. It has been used by colleges of education and teacher preparation programs since forever (well, technically, it was published in 1956 by Benjamin Bloom and associates). Seriously, I've traveled across the country training teachers, and every time, I ask for those not familiar with Bloom's Taxonomy to raise their hands. I have yet to have one teacher raise their hands. For that reason, this part of the book will not be focused on what most teachers have already received training and resources on (creating Higher Order Thinking Questions vs. Lower Order Thinking Questions). Instead, as I do in my FRESH Workshops, I will take this time to challenge teachers to think in a new way about how FRESH classrooms take the idea of higher-order connections outside of the school and into the communities and lived realities of students.

In the Engagement section of the book, I discussed student-to-community engagement as one essential part of a more holistic approach to student engagement. In that section, I mentioned that as a principal, I required each of my teachers to include a community connection to each curricular unit they planned throughout the school year. This connection could mean either taking the students into the community to participate in a new learning experience or bringing in someone from the community to the school to facilitate a unique learning experience.

Due to state testing and school budget constraints, many educators simply wait until the end of the academic year before taking students anywhere. Even then, those field trips may be more fun-centered experiences that reward select groups of students for their excellent behavior records or academic achievements over the school year. Community member's invitations into the schools are also many times narrowly limited to more non-academic events like career day or a guest appearance for a read-aloud. While I am not suggesting that these traditional approaches are irrelevant, I believe there are many opportunities to dig deeper that simply don't get tapped in most conventional learning environments.

In the FRESH Classroom, educators start to push the content connections to the next level by designing learning experiences that are transformative for students and empower community members to feel more valued and welcomed into the school. This is bigger than PTA programs and photo ops because it's about community empowerment.

WHAT DO HIGHER-ORDER LEARNING EXPERIENCES LOOK LIKE IN REAL LIFE?

From the Page to the Stage

I told you earlier I still remember asking my AP English IV teacher, "Are there no Black people in Britain?" when we had to choose a research subject from a long list of old, dead, White men, I also remember the culminating part of the drama unit that was our trip to see a play. I still remember falling in love with the stage watching Shakespeare's "Hamlet" come to life. It was the production, more so than the plot itself, that left me spell bound. The elaborate costumes, the sprawling set design with moving parts, and the commanding presence of the actors all created a transformative learning experience for me and my classmates. It brought the genre to life. I know that because all these years later, I'll never forget my first time at the theater. My teacher would have been well within the confines of her contract to simply assign us a play to read in class, take our reading quiz, and keep it moving. But her commitment to unlocking new experiences and going the extra mile not only impacted us, as her students, but also her legacy of excellence continued within me when I became a high school English teacher.

We always had a drama unit, and after reading and analyzing plays by other authors and writing our own, I continued the tradition that my AP English teacher started. I took my students to the Dallas Theatre Center to see the genre come to life in various productions including "A Christmas Carol," "To Kill a Mockingbird," and others. I took my students as a teacher, then as a principal, to see plays on the stage. This connection involved using the unit from the book for empowering them to see how and where these skills were meaningful in real life. In their day-to-day lives, learning about stage directions and character development may seem abstract and irrelevant, especially when some have never seen a play. Seeing all these moving parts come together on the stage, in person, gave them an opportunity for a hands-on connection with content.

While I don't discount the use of videos during instruction, there's something different happening at the point of making a human connection (the reason modern technology has never replaced live theater). Students were not only learning the content; they were learning the social skills required for interacting in a new environment. Despite sometimes having some of the most behaviorally challenging students go to the theater, as I told you before, I never had a student embarrass themselves (or their family names, as I so eloquently told them) by acting out during a production. This was one of my favorite points of connection in one of my least favorite units.

Stephanie Boyce
November 27, 2012 · 👥
My crazy students at the theater today... So well behaved and intelligent!
#thetigerway #educator http://instagr.am/p/SjOF_omDsu/

From the Projector to the Garden Project

When I was a principal, I would review my teachers' weekly lesson plans (completed Google slides ready to present to students) and provide them feedback in real-time. I'll never forget reviewing a science lesson with a first-year science teacher who was super passionate about the work but still in need of coaching. In this particular lesson activity, the teacher explained the different types of leaves. She had inserted pictures of various leaves in the slide for students to see and compare. I quickly noticed that the kind of leaves she showed could be found outside on the grounds of our school. I asked her if there was a reason why the lesson couldn't include time for the students to go out and gather leaves around the building. She paused for a second, then, as if I had opened some door and granted her access to walk into a new realm, she accepted my recommendation, updated the lesson plan, and from then on, "Nature Walks" became a regular staple in her science classroom.

This may sound like a small thing for some, but it was the beginning of years of innovation in the classroom for that teacher. Because the expectation was set that we would get students up, out, and connected to the world as often as possible, this teacher led the way for her team. One of the most memorable projects I can recall from her class was a classroom garden project for 6th-grade students.

After identifying a space on the grounds for the actual garden, this teacher knew she would have to include a community connection to the unit, so she contacted the Dallas Arboretum and Botanical Gardens and planned a trip for students to see and learn about some of the most beautifully elaborate gardens in the area. For many of the students, this was their first trip to the Arboretum. Although it was a scorcher outside (in true Texas fashion), they observed many gardens with various types of flowers and plants and arrangements. The teacher was able to connect organically with their observations and teach them about organisms and environments.

The next part of the Classroom Garden Project included the teacher strategically reaching out to local businesses near the school to solicit their support for resources to make the project possible. Sure enough, companies like Home Depot, Lowe's, Calloway's nursery, etc., responded to her requests for support and donated the materials necessary for the students to be hands-on in the garden and creating. The key to success here was writing a letter that was inclusive of the learning objectives students would be working toward and giving the companies a time by which she needed to know if they would be able to support the activity, and if so, in what capacity. Educators should never take for granted that local businesses may have a lot going on in their internal day-to-day operations because most of them are willing to partner with schools, especially when it gets them a good photo op and a shout out from your campus or district publicly. Let them know they will receive all of that when they accept your offer to support kids in their upcoming projects.

Lastly, this project came back full circle by including an authentic judge for the Classroom Garden projects, the representative from the Dallas Arboretum and Botanical Gardens who led the students in their day of learning when they visited at the beginning of the unit. I'd like to think these types of opportunities are beneficial not just to the students but also to the community partner that gets to see the span of their impact from their daily work to an actual classroom where students are impacted in a meaningful way. I was proud to see their finished classroom garden. Also, I was in awe of the process they went through to use their hands and collaborate together to build something great. They were peacock proud!

From the Big Screen to the Classroom

One of my favorite things was to take students to the movies for educationally valuable lessons. Most major motion pictures begin to make a buzz, years if not months, in advance of release dates, giving educators plenty of time to prepare connections to lesson plans. My favorite one, to date, was the premiere of the movie "Hidden Figures." After explaining to the science and math teachers the historical significance of the upcoming film, they made connections from the units on force, motion, and energy to the movie, to iFly indoor skydiving, and to the Space Center in Houston. This allowed us to extend the learning to our end-of-year trip to Houston for this group of students. Sounds like a lot, huh? It was a lot to plan, but the students and staff all had a great time in the end.

The key here, as with much instructional heavy lifting, is teamwork. For instance, a couple of teachers may have been running point on the content specifics and aligning the assignments students completed at each stop to the standards. The administrative assistant was doing the logistics of planning and solidifying the hotel and bus specifics as well as securing payments from families, etc. As the administrator supervising the trip, I manned the extra-ness of the journey. Yes, I do invent words—I earned the right.

For example, when we scheduled dinner at a popular pizza spot in Houston, I coordinated with professionals from various fields (i.e., a doctor, lawyer, entrepreneur, scientist, etc.) to meet us and chat with students about their various fields and answer questions the students had about what they did for a living. I also managed to fit in self-guided tours at two colleges (Texas Southern University and The University of Houston) while we were there so that the 5th and 6th-grade students could see what a college campus looked and felt like given that many of them had never been on a college campus before. The one night that we stayed at the hotel, I planned a pool-side pizza party for the kids to enjoy before they had to retire for the night. It was so much to coordinate logistically, but it was worth it, and they were too worn out to even think about causing trouble in the hotel that evening. LOL.

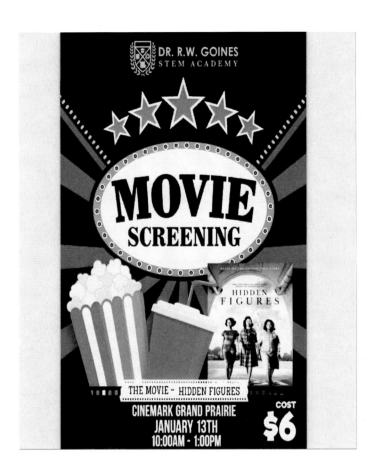

The Government in Real Life

When the English and social studies teachers partnered to teach students about the branches of government and how government functions, we naturally waded into our community connections in multiple ways.

1. Teachers reached out to both the Republican and Democratic campaign offices (this was the election year of 2016) to see if they would allow students to learn more about what they do and how campaigns worked by objectively explaining logistics, not pushing partisan platforms. After only receiving an invite from the Democratic campaign office in Fort Worth, a group of 5th-grade students went to that campaign office and learned from local organizers how campaigns run in real-time.

2. In connection with this unit, I also took a group of Student Government Association students to our local university, The University of Texas at Arlington, to meet the officers of the Student Congress and learn more about student leadership roles in college. They also stayed to observe the weekly meeting, as hopeful Student Congress candidates gave their campaign speeches for elected positions. This trip also, quite organically, included a self-guided tour of the university.

3. We also took a 1-day trip to Austin, TX, for a Capitol Tour. This trip has become a staple for 5th-grade students in Texas, so this was not a trip that required much detail. They did the standard Capitol tour that was followed by a tour of the University of Texas. If you're counting, that's the fourth university campus tour I'm mentioning 5th and 6th-grade students had access to in a single school year. Despite the state's best efforts at ensuring college and career readiness, there is nothing more beneficial than getting kids' feet and eyeballs on those lush green lawns. Nothing was better than letting them eat in the food court, feel the buzz of bustling college students heading to a lecture hall, witness the chatting of friends playing Frisbee in a green area, or even better, seeing a frat or sorority set off a step on the main stage. These trips are the passport to college access these students might not get otherwise!

4. Additionally, we launched campaigns for Student Government officer positions. We saw students deploy posters on the walls, hand out flyers with all kinds of tantalizing treats, and state their cases with prepared speeches before the student body. In the end, they all cast their votes for the candidates they felt would represent them the best.

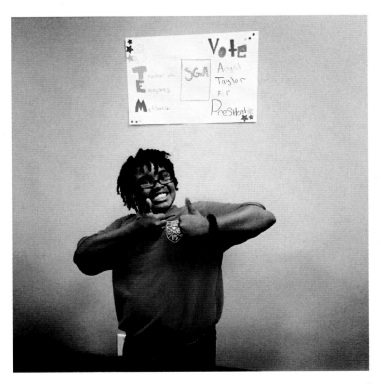

5. Lastly, on election day in 2016, the students cast their votes for President of the United States (after watching the presidential debates throughout the unit and analyzing each party's platform as part of their assignments).

Police, from Community to Campus

Another one of the most valuable community connections occurred when the ELAR teacher used a unit focused thematically around community heroes to have officers from the Dallas County Sherriff's Department come to the campus. As the planning for this day was underway, we experienced real-life opposition by some students, when one young man, a 6th grader who was aware of the shooting deaths of Alton Sterling and Philando Castille at the hands of police officers in the Summer of 2016 as well as of the social unrest that followed asked the ELAR teacher, "If police are heroes, why are they always killing Black men?"

This question was the consequence of the critical culture I encouraged, as a principal, and the safe spaces teachers allowed for such authentic questions to emerge.

Instead of shutting the student down with some cliché, utopian response, like "That's only some police officers, and most officers are your friends," we leaned into this teachable moment. I gave the green light for that teacher to allow students to share their concerns and what they knew (both the substantiated and unsubstantiated opinions), and we created a safe space for them to discuss their feelings. Next, we had the students research the facts and think deeply about a very emotionally driven discussion topic for many people. Students had to learn how to process the emotions tied to discrimination against people of color and get to the numbers and equip themselves with knowledge, as emerging scholars.

By the day the officers arrived on campus, the students had prepared the questions they wanted to ask (we typically fielded them in advance to ensure students crafted thoughtful questions and didn't embarrass us, let's be honest). That one student who dared to speak his truth from the beginning was prepared to ask the officers his question about why Black men were disproportionately at the receiving end of lethal force and police brutality in America. To this day, I cannot tell you what the officer's response to that question was. I remember it was something polite anyone would expect from a cop speaking to a 6th-grade student, but what I remember is the process of validating that student's lived experience. I think about how his voiced concern could have been swept under the rug or even dismissed within the confines of a culturally disconnected classroom by a teacher who allowed their personal positions to blind them from the realities students encounter daily.

The truth is by growing up in communities of color and in suburban areas (as I was a migrant student who lived all around the DFW metroplex), I saw firsthand how disconnected and mean-spirited many cops could be when handling people in the hood, versus how friendly and helpful they were with White people in the suburbs. Mind-boggling. Having the chance to create a safe space on the campus to allow students to have a friendly interaction with law enforcement officers while being honest in their interactions was a big win in my mind.

The day went well. The K9 unit was even there, and after having my social studies teacher volunteer to get into the fat suit for the K9 demonstration, we all looked on in complete amazement as the officer, giving the dog a verbal command, sent him in a full sprint across the gym floor toward the social studies teacher at the other end of the gym ready for a tussle. *Let me pause here to reassure you I was totally aware that this could either end up being one of the most incredible things the students had ever observed at school, or the teacher would end up lambasted, and I'd be fired immediately.* The

German Shepard launched at the teacher, grabbing the arm of the fat suit in a death grip. Despite the fight that ensued, the teacher stayed on his feet, refusing to be pulled to the ground by the dog. The gym erupted in cheers as the students, now entirely impressed by the teacher's athletic ability, roared his name and cheered him on!

As swiftly as his words had unleashed the fury of that dog on the teacher, the officer shouted another command, and that dog released our fearless teacher at once! The crowd went wild, once again, as the teacher raised his hands, proclaiming victory, while the students cheered like he'd just gone 12 rounds with Muhammad Ali. It was another classic moment. Another example of how the teachers' commitment to making community connections led to experiences the books and videos on projector screens could never produce.

Did we still have to facilitate the necessary conversations with students about how to safely interact with law enforcement officers when they are out in the real world? Yes. But equally as important, we brought them into close proximity with officers (some of them for the first time) and told them why they shouldn't be afraid, why they should be respectful, why some officers find themselves fearful in certain situations, and when and where it's appropriate to speak truth to power. The goal was not just for students to read about "community heroes" in the pages of books and mindlessly ingest the author's ideas but to understand that nuance exists between individuals and institutions in the community.

Nursing Home Visit ... Authentic Hugs Wanted!

In an ELAR unit with a story that explored a kid losing a grandparent and the importance of our elders in society, a group of students visited a local nursing home as their community connection. Since it was the holiday season, the Student Government members volunteered to conduct a clothing drive to collect items needed at the nursing home. Then they went to visit with the elderly residents and delivered the things they had collected that month. In the end, the residents didn't want the students to leave. It was the only visit some of them had received in a while.

Community Connections ... Just for the Good of It!

In addition to the community, real-world connections directly linked to content and project objectives, some experiences were just for the good of connecting. I'll share a couple of those with you as well.

Etiquette Lessons

Each year, since I started mentoring young ladies in my Act Like a Lady, Think Like a Boss mentorship group at the high school level, I took a group of students to the local Pappadeaux Seafood Kitchen. During this trip, the restaurant's general manager (one of the only women with that title in that food chain) gave students etiquette lessons for successfully navigating in a formal dining setting, and shared her professional journey in a male-dominated industry, then answered questions about running a restaurant. It became one of my favorite things to do every year, and students had a blast eating well, even dressing nicely for the occasion.

Family-Style Meals

Breaking bread with people is such a meaningful way to connect. From a Thanksgiving meal set up, family-style, with various families bringing in dishes (I know, I know, we don't want to eat food from everybody's house, you can always cater a meal), to pancakes with the Principal where my assistant and I whipped out the trusty griddles and pancake mix, a good meal works wonders. It brings us together to share space and time. It causes us to pause from our busy schedules, emails, and video chats to focus on the moment in the here and now. These were times where I sat and ate with student's families and community members. I listened to what was going on with them and received their feedback concerning how things were going with their kiddos and the school. These kinds of positive and welcoming activities made it more bearable when a difficult conversation was necessary with a parent about their student's academic or behavioral progress. We built community at the table.

Curly Girls Rock

One thing I realized about many of my Black female students was some major identity issues around beauty and hair. Whereas most students had naturally curly hair, when they occasionally had their hair straightened, everyone would "Ooo" and "Ahh" and compliment them all day about how beautiful they looked. At that time, I didn't have any children, but all I could do was think about how I was going to have a daughter one day, and I wanted those girls to know, as much as I would like my child to know, that they were fearfully and wonderfully made in the image of a God who makes no mistakes. For that reason, I was constantly complimenting their curls and trying to reassure them of their natural beauty. Ironically, I spent much of that year having my hair permanently straightened and cut into a short style that was so complicated to maintain.

Finally, I decided to accept that I needed to be the change I wanted to see in those girls. Here I was, in a position of power, and a role model to them, but I was not embracing my own natural beauty as a Black woman. My words were telling them one thing, while my actions were telling them something else. With this conviction in my heart, I decided to grow my natural hair back out and loc it. With that in mind, I planned an event, Curly Girls Rock, that would be both a celebration of the curly girls who chose to come and a tutorial on which products to use to nourish and better style their hair. I partnered with a social media influencer, who happened to be the mother of one of the students, and the owner of a local beauty supply store, who was more than happy to provide some product bags for the students to sample. Some of the young ladies expressed that they just did not know what products to use on their hair, how to detangle without damaging their hair, or even what protective styles work best for different curl patterns. The event was great and was one of the highlights of that year, for sure.

COME LEARN HOW TO LET YOUR #BLACKGIRLMAGIC GLOW!

Sometimes I know educators read about experiences like these and immediately start to brainstorm all the reasons they aren't able to do "all that extra," such as:

- I don't have enough time to plan such experiences.
- My campus/district won't fund trips.
- My students don't "know how to act."
- My class sizes are too big to go anywhere.
- My students are already behind grade level.

I want to challenge you to combat the deficit-oriented thoughts that may initially emerge with growth-minded questions that allow you to bypass traditional limitations and level-up:

- Instead of thinking, "I don't have enough time to plan such experiences," ask, "How can I spend time at the end of this semester planning and prepping community connections for the units I will be teaching next semester?"

- Instead of thinking, "My campus/district won't fund trips," ask, "How much of my expenses may be covered by my district and campus, and which community partners would waive or reduce costs to make this learning experience a reality for my students? What fundraisers and or payment plans could I launch, far in advance, to assist students in need?"

- Instead of thinking, "My students don't know how to act," ask, "What new norms and expectations will my students need in this new social/academic setting, and when should I teach those skills and have the students practice?"

- Instead of thinking, "My class sizes are too big to go anywhere," ask, "When will I take which group of students on a trip? Who in our school community (i.e., parents/guardians, campus/district-level staff members, student-teacher interns in district) could join us?"

- Instead of thinking, "My students are already behind grade level," ask, "How can I assure the learning experience and the activities are scaffolded to address the needs of the various students in my class?"

As cliché as it may sound, it's mind over matter when it comes to getting out of the box and chartering new paths. It won't be as easy as pulling out the same lesson from your saved files, but it will definitely be more rewarding. When you fix your mind on making community connections non-negotiable, then start putting one foot in front of the other heading in that direction, you're going to be blown away by how many people go out of their way to support you and your students. It's almost as if they are just waiting for the invitation, waiting to be pointed in the direction of usefulness. They want to give back to the schools and communities, especially when tied to student learning and not just donating their money for the latest fundraising effort.

You are the bridge-builder between your campus and the community. Don't wait for other teachers to jump on your bandwagon of greatness. Just pick up your tools and start building that bridge, and you'll see how even the most pessimistic teacher will be forced to pay attention to how you're changing the game. That's what FRESH Classrooms are all about! Changing the game, leveling up, and pushing on to higher heights!

References and Resources

Alber, R. (2011). *6 Scaffolding Strategies to Use With Your Students.* https://www.edutopia.org/blog/scaffolding-lessons-six-strategies-rebecca-alber

Boyce, S. (2014). *Kill the Paper Lesson Plan* [video]. https://www.youtube.com/watch?v=6fFRmm7zl5w

Langfocus. (2020). *African American Vernacular English* [video]. https://www.youtube.com/watch?v=UZpCdI6ZKU4

Lead Forward. (2021). *Resources.* https://lead4ward.com/resources//

Lyiscott, J. (2014). *Code Switching* [video]. TED. https://www.youtube.com/watch?v=k-9fmJ5xQ_mc&t=2s

Malcom X. (1964). *The Ballot or the Bullet: Speech Transcript.* https://www.rev.com/blog/transcripts/the-ballot-or-the-bullet-speech-transcript-malcolm-x

PBLWorks. (2021). *Get Started.* https://www.pblworks.org/get-started

Persaud, C. (2020). *Pedagogy: What Educators Need to Know* [Plus: 40+ Free Strategies to Implement in Your Classroom]. https://tophat.com/blog/pedagogy/

Positive Pins. (n.d.). *African Americans of STEM: STEM Posters Set.* http://www.positivepins.com/images2/blackhistory/stemposterset.jpg

Teaching Channel. (2021). *Learning Menus.* https://learn.teachingchannel.com/video/differentiating-instruction-strategy

Tomlinson, C.A. (2017). *How to Differentiate Instruction in Academically Diverse Classrooms* (3rd ed.). ASCD.

Tomlinson, C.A. *What is Differentiated Instruction?* https://www.readingrockets.org/article/what-differentiated-instruction

Tyler, The Creator. (n.d.). Nuts + Bolts Series [video]. https://www.youtube.com/re-sults?search_query=Nuts+%2B+Bolts+with+Tyler%2C+The+Creator+

Woodly, S. (2018). MC Means the Crowd: How to Spark Engagement and Motivation in Urban and Culturally Diverse Classrooms. Ideal Education Consulting, LLC.

PART III

Data Don't Lie

Chapter 11

Culturally Relevant Education

Whereas I set out to make this book more conversational in tone (even baring my journey for your entertainment), it's about to get a little formal. So, buckle up. The research on which I have built my business and dedicated my life's work deserves a little more academic maneuvering. Please allow me to put on my Dr. Boyce hat here and nerd out just a little. I'll be as concise as possible, but I know some educators that have read until this point may also be interested in the research that informed the FRESH approach. Part III is for you!

Decades' worth of research has long amplified the need for inclusive approaches to teaching students of color. The effectiveness of culturally relevant education (CRE) approaches can sustain student interest, improve academic outcomes, and improve attendance rates with those same students. CRE is not just a feel-good initiative to check off our diversity effort boxes from year to year. There are real implications to society when we under educate students in our schools, only to have them graduate and become adults.

Not only do those students tend to make less money throughout their lifetimes, but as Rychly and Graves (2012) explained, there are "projected social and civic consequences, including underemployment, health risks, lack of civic participation, and incarceration... and total annual economic burden to taxpayers because of inequity ($59.2 billion)." We all have to be concerned with creating more equitable classrooms because we are all impacted by our failure to do so. CRE is one approach that provides us a path to progress.

Derived from the multicultural education research produced in the 1990s, culturally relevant education allows teachers to combine two of the most well-known educational approaches— *culturally responsive teaching* (CRT; Gay, 2010, 2013) and *culturally relevant pedagogy* (CRP; Ladson-Billings, 1995, 2006, 2014). In addition, researchers have long labeled the various tenets of CRE in many ways, including social justice education (Esposito & Swain, 2009), reality pedagogy (Emdin, 2016), democratic science pedagogy (Basu & Barton, 2010), and culturally responsive standards-based teaching (Saifer et al., 2011). There are way too many to name here. All have been meaningful contributions to the field.

In this book, I refer to CRP, CRT, and CRSB interchangeably. CRE is used more as an umbrella term inclusive of the ideas of CRT and CRP, as they are the two most commonly discussed approaches to CRE (Aronson & Laughter, 2016). While CRT and CRP may seem similar at face value, there are nuanced differences.

Gay (2002) defined CRT as "using the cultural characteristics, experiences, and perspectives of ethnically diverse students as conduits for teaching them more effectively" (p. 106). This approach enables teachers to focus on their teaching practices in the classroom to meet their students' needs.

CRP expands those teaching practices to include concepts of social justice that extend beyond the classroom. Ladson-Billings (1995a) defined CRP as:

> A pedagogy of opposition ... committed to collective, not merely individual, empowerment. Culturally relevant pedagogy rests on three criteria or propositions: (a) Students must experience academic success; (b) students must develop and/or maintain cultural competence; and (c) students must develop a critical consciousness through which they challenge the status quo of the current social order. (p. 160)

CRP, then, requires teachers to enter the recursive process of acknowledging their own attitudes, dispositions, and worldviews because they may hold beliefs that conflict with those of their students. By acknowledging their personal values and beliefs, teachers can attempt to reconcile their perspectives with their students' values and viewpoints as they work toward bridging gaps in achievement for the students of color they serve.

For example, non-CRP teachers may use language that classifies their students' preferred musical genre as academically irrelevant because it may clash with the teachers' own cultural inclination. Meanwhile, CRP-oriented teachers may challenge themselves to be open to and inclusive of the cultural differences they experience with diverse students by asking these students to discuss what they find appealing about their musical tastes (Milner, 2012). Despite their specific differences, both CRP and CRT are pedagogical tools used by CRE-oriented teachers to ground classrooms and promote social justice and educational equality (Aronson & Laughter, 2016).

Thus, CRE-oriented teachers reject the idea of teaching any standardized, one-size-fits-all curriculum developed according to the dominant culture's values. Culturally responsive educators actively interact with diverse students based on their experiences to gain and apply new knowledge both in and out of school (Rychly & Graves, 2012). My best advice to educators is to not get so hung up on the semantics and labels that we miss the heart of the matter and, in that, miss opportunities for real professional growth that dismantles injustice and ensures social justice.

Chapter 12

CRE and Teachers

Much research has been done to examine the link between teachers' pedagogical approaches and the role culturally relevant education has in improving teachers' instructional effectiveness in the classroom with students of color, in particular (Bonner & Adams, 2012; Brown & Crippen, 2016; Esposito & Swain, 2009; Johnson, 2011; Milner, 2011). Based on the findings from these studies, educators are encouraged to focus on four things in order to effectively adopt CRE practices: (a) rejecting deficit perspectives to build cultural competence, (b) aligning culture and academic standards, (c) cultivating consciousness, and (d) promoting culturally proficient learning communities. This section synthesizes the research findings that are specifically centered around these items, which researchers consider essential when studying teachers' implementation of culturally responsiveness in their classrooms.

Rejecting Deficit Perspectives to Build Cultural Competence

In order for issues of achievement to be addressed, it is necessary to redefine the paradigm educators use to assess students of color. Irvine (2010) suggested that the idea of an achievement gap is nothing more than the manifestation of other gaps that have gone unaddressed by educators. One such gap is the low expectations and deficit mindsets many educators may have concerning students of color. With this assertion in mind, Milner (2012) explained that while most teachers attempt to teach all students, they sometimes lower expectations with students who resist or show opposition to the mainstream culture. In these situations, many teachers allow students to sit in their classrooms without providing engaging educational experiences for them.

CRE teachers reject such deficit mindsets and work to better understand the cultural capital their students already possess. Cultural capital refers to the knowledge, values, and ideas developed across generations in families and communities (Al-Fadhli & Kersen, 2010). By failing to recognize the benefits of cultural capital, teachers may inadvertently devalue their students' "culture, knowledge, language, tastes, and dispositions" (Saltman, 2014, p. 7) as a form of *symbolic violence*. In the classrooms of students of color, symbolic violence of this sort is a phenomenon experienced too often.

Studies conducted by Ladson-Billings (1995a), Milner (2012), and Irvine (2010) illustrated how teachers' use of CRE helped to shift the perspectives of the teachers and help them better understand students of color. Yosso (2005) extended the concept of cultural capital arguing that *cultural wealth* forms from the capital created by the shared experiences that occur in communities of color. Yosso called this unique set of knowledge and skills, Community Cultural Wealth (CCW) and listed the six types of CCW capital as "(1) aspirational, (2) navigational, (3) social, (4) linguistic, (5) familial, and (6) resistant capital" (p. 244). Yosso (2005) originally defined these six forms of capital as follows:

1. *Aspirational capital* is directly associated with the capacity to hold on to hope even in situations that seem to create insurmountable obstacles. This capital equips people in communities of color to understand the real and perceived barriers that exist in society and continue to strive for more, nonetheless.
2. *Linguistic capital* refers to the fact that many students of color "arrive at school with multiple language and communication skills" (p. 78). Being bilingual affords these students benefits their monolingual counterparts do not receive. Visual art, music, and poetry are also included as forms of linguistic capital.
3. *Familial capital* finds value in the communal relationships that exist in communities of color. From the rich histories, oral traditions,

unity, and even the adopting of community members into pseudo families, these relationships and the resources tied to them are highly valued.

4. *Social capital* refers to the skills provided by others to help one navigate through various societal institutions. This capital manifests in the form of emotional or instrumental support. This obligation for people in these communities to "lift as [they] climb" is a big part of how social capital is accumulated (p. 80).

5. *Navigational capital* requires a certain level of mental dexterity to maneuver through institutions that were not created for people of color. While systematic racism is engrained in many of the institutions that exist in our country, navigational capital sheds light on the importance of independence when moving through various institutions.

6. *Resistant capital* denotes the "skills fostered through oppositional behavior that challenges inequality" (p. 81). This aspect of cultural wealth implies that individuals realize the bigger implications of racist institutions and they fight against them. Those who possess resistant capital seek to change the structures they resist.

When educators take time to reframe the way they perceive students' cultural capital and broaden that definition to include their students' experiences, they position themselves to better understand the strengths of the students they serve and build upon those strengths.

In addition to teachers understanding students' cultural capital, one of the most respected authorities on culturally relevant pedagogy, Ladson-Billings (1995a, 1995b), highlighted the importance of educators committing to CRE in order to build student's cultural competence. She (1995a) studied eight highly effective teachers of African American students over the course of three years. These teachers were nominated as outstanding educators by parents or principals because of their lower numbers of office referrals, higher levels of student attendance, and higher standardized test scores. Ladson-Billings (1995a) conducted interviews, observed classrooms, and videotaped classroom instruction to collect data and found that the participants worked to build the cultural competence of their students.

The term, cultural competence, refers to one's ability to retain their authenticity while working to gain new learning. One way to understand this idea is to consider that assimilating into traditional school environments is oftentimes referred to as "acting White" (Ladson-Billings, 1995a, p. 160), which is socially frowned upon by many students of color.

Additionally, everything from their preferred way of dressing or speaking can be misunderstood by teachers. For this reason, teachers have to be keenly aware of how they view the varied strengths their students bring into their classrooms and work to build up their sense of pride in themselves and their communities. While expanding teachers' understanding of students is a step in the right direction, CRE teachers go a step further by overtly helping students of color foster a sense of acceptance and pride for their own culture (Ladson-Billings, 1995a). Otherwise, teachers might inadvertently devalue their student's potential.

Despite their campus adopting scripted lessons that made it difficult for teachers to make the content personally meaningful and relevant to their specific students, Esposito and Swain (2009) reported that the seven teachers they interviewed committed to using culturally relevant pedagogy in their classrooms as a means to ensure students saw their needs reflected in the classroom. For instance, one teacher ensured her students saw images of positive African-American role models on the walls of the classroom even if the school did not provide funds for such things. Another teacher took time to address stereotypes students had about Africa and, in turn, their own ancestry to challenge the misconceptions they held. These teachers illustrate the power of the CRE classroom to build students' cultural competence and transform their own conceptions of self in the process. While this idea of building cultural competence includes students understanding their own culture, it also refers to educators taking time to understand the differences between the students and themselves and how those differences play out in classrooms (Esposito & Swain, 2009; Milner 2012).

For instance, one Black teacher in Esposito and Swain's (2009) study acknowledged that her middle-class upbringing meant she had different cultural experiences than the students she served in the low-income area. These differences have the potential to cause conflicts in classrooms if teachers are unaware of how their own cultural identities may affect their students and the pedagogical decisions they make on a daily basis. CRE teachers must commit to continuous and recursive reflection to ensure they are always working to better understand and uplift the students they serve, no matter how similar or different their cultural backgrounds.

Another such teacher is detailed in Milner's (2011) 2-year case study of a White male science teacher's classroom in a diverse, urban school in the southeastern region of the United States. After conducting classroom observations, analysis of unspecified documents and artifacts, and multiple interviews with the science teacher, Milner (2011) noted that as the teacher built cultural understanding of his students, he became more culturally responsive and more effective. For example, as he developed meaningful relationships with the students, he realized this gave him greater insight into their specific needs. He also found it necessary to also share more of his own story with them. As a result, he built a mutual trust with his students. In the end, this teacher came to a deeper knowledge of himself and how his worldview impacted his practice.

While some educators view their personal backgrounds and culture as irrelevant to teaching content, this study's findings indicated that educators who work to build their students' cultural identities through the use of CRE actually build their own cultural competence in the process.

Rejecting deficit perspectives enabled researchers to reveal how under-standing the varied forms of cultural capital students possess and building up students' cultural competence, which are the key elements of CRE, are necessary steps to engage and uplift their students.

Aligning Culture and Academic Standards

In the studies that follow, authors argue that it is not enough for teachers to appeal only to the cultural interests of students of color, they must also ensure the rigor incorporated by the performance standards to increase student achievement (Bonner & Adams, 2012; Brown & Crippen, 2016; Ellis et al., 2017; Hernandez, Morales, & Shroyer, 2013; Johnson, 2011; Ladson-Billings, 1995a). More specifically, Saifer, Edwards, Ellis, Ko, and Stuczynski (2011) explained culturally responsive teaching addresses "the needs of students by improving motivation and engagement, and standards-based teaching provides all students with the opportunity for rigorous, high-level learning. Culturally Responsive Standards-Based (CRSB) teaching means doing both, together" (p. 4). The marriage of these two ideas is the key to teachers' effective use of CRE strategies.

Effective implementation of CRE in science and math requires that teachers reject the myth of context-neutrality in these fields and find ways to consider both their students' interests and the content standards (Bonner & Adams, 2012; Brown & Crippen, 2016; Ellis et al., 2017; Hernandez et al., 2013; Ladson-Billing, 1995; Milner, 2012). Milner (2012) explained the context-neutral mindsets of some teachers as potentially troubling because educators and students live in social contexts; therefore, there exists a need to consider issues through students' perspectives. When teachers attempt to remain impartial in their approach, they forfeit the opportunity to address the realities of their schools and communities.

Illustrating this idea, Brown and Crippen (2016) interviewed five high school science teachers, conducted classroom observations, and collected artifacts (i.e., lesson study reports) to gain insights into the implementation of culturally responsive science practices in their classrooms. After the teachers participated in a 6-month long professional development entitled, Science Teachers are Responsive to Students (STARTS), in which a portion of the training was dedicated to teaching the teachers about the essentials of implementing CRE in their science classes, the teachers implemented the CRE lessons they created with a group of culturally diverse students.

In the end, Brown and Crippen (2016) found that effective implementation of CRE in science required teachers to learn about their students in order to incorporate the students' experiences and interests in the science lessons. These findings revealed the importance of teachers being intentional about cultivating a strong knowledge of students' cultural backgrounds and the need to tie those interests into the science curriculum.

Other researchers also found the importance of making these connections. For instance, Mensah (2011) conducted a qualitative study into how three pre-service science teachers planned and executed a culturally responsive pollution unit. Using observations, interviews, informal conversations, and lesson plans as data sources, Mensah (2011) concluded that the implementation of culturally responsive teaching in the science class depended on the teachers' ability to make real-world connections to the content (e.g., impacts of pollution) as well as to students' personal interests (e.g., how such pollution impacts their community) in the lessons they brought to the classroom.

In order for these things to happen, she noted that teachers must be trained to align culture and content in deep and meaningful ways. Hernandez et al. (2013) also conducted a qualitative study focused on defining the essential practices in culturally responsive math and science classes. After observing 12 preservice teachers' implementation of their lessons, they found that one of the most impactful practices was the ability to successfully integrate the cultural interests of students with the course content.

While the previous studies focused specifically on Science, Technology, Engineering, and Math (STEM) subjects, the following research explores the use of CRE in other subjects and further demonstrates the impact of aligning culture and content in CRE classrooms. For example, Ladson-Billing (1994, 1995a, 2006, 2014) highlighted how important it is for students to see their backgrounds included as part of course content as a means of affirming the importance of their culture in the learning process. For example, in one study, Ladson-Billings (1995a) reported how several reading teachers accomplished this task. She noted how one reading teacher used student-selected rap lyrics to teach poetry while another instructor welcomed parents to come in and teach students different life and job skills.

Another teacher allowed students to speak their home languages in class but taught them how to speak standard English as well, because this ability might be important to their future success. This skill is referred to as "code-switching" (p. 161), a term used to explain knowing the appropriate time to use an idiom, colloquialism, or language as opposed to totally using academic English. This effort to align students' pre-existing knowledge and cultural experiences with the new knowledge provided by school curriculum is the quintessential essence of successful CRE teachers.

Cultivating Consciousness

Despite restrictive educational reforms, culturally relevant education (CRE) requires teachers to equip students to become conscious combatants of the injustices that impact society (Esposito & Swain, 2009; Hernandez et al., 2013; Ladson-Billings, 1995a). *Critical consciousness*, explained Ladson-Billings (1995a), is the idea that culturally relevant pedagogy must empower students to operate "beyond those individual characteristics of academic achievement and cultural competence, students must develop a broader ... consciousness that allows them to critique ... institutions that produce and maintain social inequities" (p. 162).

Teachers who participated in this seminal study had their civics students write letters to officials about community issues. This type of activity promoted a sense of critical consciousness that moved students toward thinking of themselves as agents of change. Notably, before teachers could create these learning opportunities, they had to reflect and commit to implementing such practices that were not included in the standard lesson plans found in the textbooks. This is a practice shared by teachers committed to CRE, which sets the focus of the teachers' practices outside the confines of the classroom and on to impactful change in communities.

Esposito and Swain (2009) similarly found that this appeal to sociopolitical consciousness is a commonly used teacher practice when studying culturally responsive educators. *Sociopolitical consciousness* refers to the teacher's ability to teach students to think critically about the curriculum and the world around them. One example, briefly mentioned previously, would be the Pledge Activity. Instead of just requiring the students to stand and recite the Pledge of Allegiance, one of the teachers in this specific study designed an assignment requiring students to analyze the declarations made in it and how "one nation under God, indivisible... and justice for all" apply to Black people in America (Esposito & Swain, 2009). Exercises like this required the teachers to push themselves out of the confines of the scripted curricula and encourage students to think critically about themselves and the world around them.

Further, Esposito and Swain (2009) argued that effective CRE teachers not only encourage students to become more conscious of the inequalities that surround them, but also these teachers instill a *sense of agency*, which refers to students' feelings of autonomy and self-efficacy when confronted with the truth of social injustice. The researchers stated that, to achieve this goal, educators should not treat students as victims of their circumstances but should empower them to be change agents in their communities.

When hearing students share stories of difficult life experiences, instead of responding with pity, the participating teachers challenged the students with questions, such as "How can we change this?" (Esposito & Swain, 2009, p. 42). By asking this type of question, teachers enable students to have a sense of autonomy for their own academic success and the success of their communities.

The importance of instilling agency was an idea further supported by Hernandez et al. (2013), who studied 12 pre-service teachers through their math and science classes to their final student teaching classes. They collected data through interviews, observations, and analysis of artifacts (i.e., lesson plans, teacher self-reflections, philosophy of teaching). The researchers determined that each teacher had illustrated evidence of implementing culturally responsive lessons. They did this by advocating for their students and constructing learning opportunities that enabled them to challenge their systems and world views. The teachers also used real-world examples of scientific and mathematical concepts, modeling, related their backgrounds to their students, built on students' background knowledge, hands-on activities, and incorporated the native language of the students (Hernandez et al., 2013).

While teachers' approaches may vary, their ability to cultivate the students' consciousness is an essential characteristic of CRE classrooms. This consciousness allows students to better understand the importance of being good citizens and empowers them to understand how they may impact the world.

Culturally Proficient Learning Communities

Whereas the earlier sections focused on what teachers can do in the classroom to contribute to student success, Lindsey et al. (2009) concentrated on teacher supports that can lay the foundation for more effective classroom pedagogy. They found, for CRE to be effective, teachers needed time to form communities with other teachers to discuss student data, plan lessons together, and engage in professional dialogue during the school day, such as through shared planning periods (Woodland, 2016). This view contradicts the traditional view that teachers are independent professionals, with autonomous control of their classes (Lortie, 2002) and having little time for collaboration with colleagues (Mayer & Phillips, 2012).

This perspective has gained popularity due to research on best practices in teaching (Colbert, 2010; Reeves, Hung, & Sun, 2017; Rinke, 2009; Woodland, 2016). In fact, despite the myriad names ascribed to this concept of teacher collaboration (e.g., team meetings, departmental meetings, collaboration time, professional learning communities), professional learning communities (PLC) have emerged as one of the most widely accepted strategies for teacher collaboration in PK-12 schools. While its implementation may look different in practice, the power of the PLC to impact student achievement has been the focus of many researchers (e.g., Lindsey, Jungwirth, Pahl, & Lindsey, 2009; Rinke, 2009; Vescio, Ross, & Adams, 2008).

For example, Woodland (2016) suggested that at the core of the PLC process teachers focus on the following essential questions to ensure effectiveness:

> (1) What should our students know, understand, and be able to do? (2) How will we know what and when our students have learned? and (3) What should we keep, stop, and/or start doing to ensure that students who don't learn, AND students who do learn, continue to make meaningful progress? (p. 507)

Put simply, Goodlad, Mantle-Bromley, and Goodlad (2004) suggested rigorous PLCs must include dialogue, decision-making, action, and evaluation. This four-step process offers a more straightforward path for PLC implementation in schools and allows educators to engage in meaningful discussions focused on both student achievement and the instructional approaches created to help students reach learning goals.

While this structure is a strong start toward increasing teachers' intentionality and collective accountability, the strength of an effective PLC lies in the willingness of its members to participate in the process (Ronfeldt et al., 2015). For that reason, a team of teachers who fail to understand and/or connect to the culture of the students they serve could become accustomed to recycling ineffective teaching practices, if they fail to include the elements of cultural proficiency in their PLC process (Colbert, 2010).

Lindsey et al. (2009) regarded "cultural proficiency as a frame for communities of learners to intentionally focus on setting and reaching academic achievement goals for students who have historically not been well served by schools" (p. 4). Where many PLCs might place the focus on teacher collaboration and instructional strategies, adding a culturally proficient lens to these meetings requires teachers to reflect on contexts beyond the data and numbers and challenge their own thinking and approaches to pedagogy as a team (Lindsey et al., 2009). Lindsey et al. (2009) provided the example of a school district working to incorporate the following five essential elements of culturally proficient practices: (a) assessing cultural knowledge, (b) valuing diversity, (c) managing the dynamics of difference, (d) adapting to diversity, and (e) institutionalizing cultural knowledge.

As a part of its improvement plan, the district focused on using *culturally proficient learning communities* as a means to rethink how they approached matters of diversity and improving student achievement. This plan required "a shift from the language of blaming the students and their circumstances to the language of personal responsibility for teaching and learning" (Lindsey et al., 2009, p. 58). In addition to collecting and analyzing data in education, Lindsey et al. (2008) promoted connecting with students and their families and working to become more culturally proficient as the key to increasing the instructional effectiveness of professional learning communities. Similarly, Ndunda, Sickle, Perry, and Capelloni (2017) found a positive impact on student learning when math and science teachers at a low-income urban school worked together to include culturally relevant approaches to instruction.

Ndunda et al. (2017) noted that three themes emerged as essential: an ethics of care, teacher agency, and aesthetics of professional interactions. An *ethics of care* referred to the teachers desire to support each other in an effort to better serve students. When teachers saw a positive impact on their

149

students, they were more likely to seek and try more strategies as a team. *Teacher agency* referred to the teachers' collective view of themselves as change agents. As the teachers experienced success in their classrooms, they began to feel more empowered as professionals. *Aesthetics of professional interactions* referred to the PLC members being openly vulnerable with each other and willing to take risks alongside each other. All three themes played an important role with the PLC team as they worked to be more culturally proficient in their math and science classes. As a result of their efforts, the math assessments indicated 15% of the students had basic math skills at the onset of the study, and by the end of the PLC intervention, 50% of them had mastered the standards. Likewise, in science, after the 15-week PLC intervention 70% to 92% of students were passing the science assessment, as opposed to the 11% pass rate at the onset of the study. These outcomes showed how a focus on culturally responsive PLC implementation can be used to positively impact teachers' instructional effectiveness in their classrooms.

Consequently, from the seminal work of Ladson-Billings (1994, 1995a) to the more contemporary studies of CRE in recent years (Brown & Crippen, 2016; Ellis et al., 2017; Hernandez et al., 2013; Lindsey et al., 2009; Ndunda et al., 2017), research affirms the positive impact of CRE on teaching practices and student achievement. These studies postulated that CRE teachers working toward rejecting deficit perspectives to build cultural competence, aligning culture and academic standards, fostering the social consciousness of their students, and engaging in culturally proficient learning communities are essential partners in improving instructional effectiveness of students of color (Bonner & Adams, 2012, Lindsey et al., 2009; Yosso, 2005). While CRE practices can be beneficial to teachers' perceptions of practice and cultural understanding, the following section highlights the importance of CRE in STEM classrooms specifically.

Bill Nye, Boy Bye

(Because Representation Matters)

"Little girls need to have more role models... that are recent, and not just notable historical figures from the past, so that kids can have examples to follow and not just remember."
~ Hannah Pals

The title of this insert may sound rude initially, but it's no shade to Bill Nye (I was simply trying to rhyme, and Beyoncé was front of mind... per usual). The truth is I cannot think of one scientist I ever learned about during my PreK-12 years that looked like me. Perhaps George Washington Carver, as a Black man. All that I knew about science was presented in textbooks or illustrated through media. Hence, the reason Bill Nye ended up in the title above. He is, in my mind, the iconic scientist. Even saying the word, scientist conjures up imagery of a slender White man with wiry gray hairs standing atop his head while adorning the white coat. I see him in his chemistry lab perched behind a table, drowning in test tubes, glass beakers, and Bunson burners. Can you see him? I bet you can. He's the default image we were given.

Unfortunately for me, and many children that look like me, this lack of representation also led to a lack of interest in science. I mean how uncool is it to be a scientist? Imagine my surprise when I got older and started to see images of scientists, doctors, lab technicians, and others dressed in plain clothes (even rocking Js) in all shades of Black and Brown, just like me. It blew my mind.

Shows like Nuts + Bolts with Tyler, the Creator who spent each episode learning how some of his favorite things were made (like furniture, mustard, go carts, etc.) really make science concepts approachable. Also, of note are everyday people like Branden Williams of seeds2stem.net, in Dallas, TX, where they are working to end the disparities that exist in STEM education in the community. These are scientists who literally look like they could be a relative of mine enjoying science in real life.

Sometimes, I think about how many opportunities I may have missed out on over the years by simply never being exposed to science curriculum that connected to my lived experience or community. Watching the movie Hidden Figures left me wondering what potential may have been hidden and untapped within me and so many other students who deemed science, technology, engineering, and math as uncool randomness that existed within the pages of the books we were forced to learn from—wholly disconnected from the realities of our lives. Like seriously, did the idea of dissecting a rat actually make someone think it would spark a love for science experiments in a kid? Let me assure you it did the opposite for me. I am STILL traumatized by the experience.

As the principal of a STEM academy, I ensured, with great intention, that the teachers focused on exposing our students to scientists of color and allowing students as much choice as possible in the application of STEM content. I can recall a group of 5th-grade girls diving headfirst into a project where they created their own hair care products by mixing different formulas and documenting their scientific process. After concocting the perfect recipe, they built a brand, budget, and business plan for their new products and concluded with a project presentation. Science wasn't about someone far off in a secret lab for those kids. Science was all around them and ingrained in every part of daily life.

Chapter 13

CRE and STEM

After doing this work in schools for years, one big misconception that must be addressed is the idea that STEM subjects are no place for cultural connections. Educators seem to identify ELAR, social studies, and the arts as more organically connected to CRE. Because many science and math educators believe their content area is fact-based and context neutral, they are less likely to use culturally responsive practices in their instruction. This context-neutral philosophy has led to a uniform approach to teaching science and math and contributed to decreased interest with students of color in STEM fields, which perpetuate the achievement gaps in those areas and society at large.

The lack of participation of historically underrepresented groups (i.e., Hispanics, Blacks, and women) in the STEM fields is a serious issue in the United States (National Science and Technology Council [NSTC], 2013). This problem with representation can be traced back to grade school. The ACT Corporation reported that Black and Hispanic high school students graduate significantly less prepared for college-level mathematics and science than their White counterparts. For instance, while half of the White graduates were prepared for college-level mathematics, the number decreased to 13% for Black and 27% for Hispanic high school graduates. There were similar differences in science with 47% White, 11% Black, and 21% Hispanic high school graduates with sufficient science skills (ACT, 2016b).

Subject	Black	Hispanic	White
Mathematics	13%	27%	50%
Science	11%	21%	46%
Note. Data retrieved from ACT (2016a).			

Table 1: ACT-Tested High School Graduates Meeting ACT College Readiness Benchmarks by Race

This is not just an issue that ends with K-12 classrooms. When Black and Hispanic students graduate from high school ill-equipped to perform satisfactorily at the postsecondary level, they are more likely to underachieve in college and inadvertently continue the STEM under-representation cycle in college.

Policy and educational leaders have begun to address the current shortage of Black and Hispanic Americans persisting in postsecondary STEM education to ensure that the future of innovation and creation in America is an inclusive endeavor. Since 2000, government programs and corporate partnerships have made concerted efforts to increase the participation of historically underrepresented groups in STEM (Landivar, 2013). Federal programs alone have spent upwards of $616 million in support of STEM education for these minoritized groups (NSTC, 2013).

Colleges and universities have also developed interventions to support students of color in STEM fields such as mentoring programs and targeted financial incentives and scholarships. However, the NCES (2015) reported that the disparities persist. This is evident by looking at college graduation rates from 2008 to 2013 where Whites were awarded 68% of all STEM-related bachelor's degrees followed by Asians (13%), Hispanics (9%), and Blacks (8%) (NCES, 2015). Not surprisingly, these critical gaps further extend into the workforce.

In 2011, the U.S. Census's American Community Survey data showed 71% of STEM workers were White, 15% were Asian, 7% were Hispanic, and 6% were Black (Beede et al., 2013). These numbers were disproportional to the total national population with 13% of the population Black and 18% Hispanic (US Census, 2016). This was particularly problematic because no occupational fields are projected to grow as rapidly as careers in STEM fields. The U.S. Bureau of Labor Statistics (BLS) projected that over 9 million STEM jobs would be created between 2012 and 2022 (Vilorio, 2014). These high-growth and high-salaried positions include: (a) mathematicians (median annual wage of $102,440), (b) software developers (median annual wage of $92,660), (c) biomedical engineers (median annual wage of $88,670), and (d) college biological science teachers (median annual wage of $75,740; Vilorio, 2014).

The fact that Black and Hispanic students were less likely to seek employment in these areas is a challenge for three primary reasons identified by the NSTC (2013). First, the current number of STEM workers in the United States is insufficient to handle the demands of the growing jobs in STEM fields. Second, with underrepresented groups becoming the majority in many regions of the United States, it is even more important to tap into this potential pool of professionals and equip them to work in STEM fields in the years to come. Third, the diversity of thoughts and ideas in the workforce strengthens America's innovation and contributes to the nation's competitiveness internationally.

In order to combat this cycle of underrepresentation, Snively and Corsiglia (2001) argued for educators to make science and math relevant to Black and Hispanic students. They noted that these students of color are not members of the dominant, White group and may have learning styles that diverge culturally from traditionally Western contexts of learning. As a result of these varied cultural views, researchers have studied these cultural differences and found Black and Hispanic students benefit when teachers attempt to bridge the achievement gap by using *CRE* practices (Aronson & Laughter, 2016; Gay, 2013; Ladson-Billings, 2014).

For instance, in an environmental science class, a non-CRE teacher may use examples from random rivers in America to make a point about the impact of pollution on communities; however, a CRE teacher might use a case concerning pollution in a river close to where the students live and have them take samples from that site to analyze and understand how that polluted river may, in fact, impact their community (Dimick, 2012). Because students live and make sense of the world from their social frames of reference, culturally responsive classrooms provide them with equity while acknowledging the value of their lived experiences.

The following section provides insight into students' perspectives concerning CRE and how CRE classrooms impacted their learning in specific subject areas.

African American Studies

(Because the truth transforms)

"African American studies is not just history. It's a composite of history, sociology, political science, psychology, the arts and religion."
-Dr. James Conyers

As a freshman at the University of Houston, I was unsure about many things, but this one thing I knew: African American Studies would be my minor (as majoring was not an option at that time). It was like learning the history of my people began to quench some deep part of my soul I never realized had been in a drought. For 4 years, they gave me a slow and steady IV drip of Nikki Giovanni, Langston Hughes, Toni Morrison, W.E.B. DuBois, August Wilson, Marcus Garvey, Malcolm X, Zora Neale Hurston, James Baldwin, Assata Shakur, Dr. Martin Luther King, Jr., and the list goes on. Each drop was hydrating my palate and creating an appetite ... for consciousness.

I'm told Historically Black Colleges and Universities (HBCUs) do a great job of this as well, but I did not attend an HBCU. So, this was the well spring I found sprouting up in the dry place. A refreshing experience for my soul. From that cup, I drank and drank and drank and developed an insatiable thirst that has not left me to this day. I read the stories and met my heroes in the pages of books and videos on screens. They were me. And I them. I let the chemically processed hair grow out of my head and rocked my natural 'fro. I challenged European beauty standards and verbally lambasted any person who came for me with my "wokeness."

I grew impatient with capitalistic notions of what I should do with my life after college. Some of my friends referred to me as a modern-day member of the Black Panther Party. It's still funny to me the way finding pride in Blackness is inherently an act of revolution to some people. On the contrary, I was undergoing an awakening. Coming to terms with the truth of America and the fullness of the roles my ancestors played in her rise to become a world superpower.

Not only had Black people been an intricate part of amassing the wealth that set this "shining city on a hill," but they had also scaled the hill, built the house, and shined their light from the inside out. They, and therefore I, were fully entitled to reap the benefits of this great country and all that her constitution promised.

In recent years, some states have added new ethnic studies courses like Mexican-American and African-American studies to their list of course offerings. I'm so excited for the high school students who will elect to take such courses and be blessed to drink from that cup before even getting to college, to have the chance to revel in the glory of their ancestors and draw strength from their unmatched resilience and immutable strivings. Teachers must recognize and acknowledge the importance of representation and truth telling. When dealing with students, some of which may be plagued by the injustices and inequities of institutional racism all around them, they need to know the stock they are made of. They need to see the faces and hear the stories they don't even know are important. The history of Black people starts way before slavery in America and the diaspora. It is the right of every child (not just the Black students) to learn the richness of that history. Because disregarding it in the pursuit of forward-focused unification does not allow for the truth that reconciliation requires.

Chapter 14

CRE and Students

Many studies have been done focusing on culturally relevant education and its impact on students, especially students of color (Basu & Barton, 2010; Boutte, Kelly-Jackson, & Johnson, 2010; Dimick, 2012; Laughter & Adams, 2012). This section discusses CRE and science, mathematics, social studies, and English/language arts classrooms. These studies shed light on the impact CRE has had on student engagement/motivation, empowerment, and academic achievement from the students' perspectives primarily. This is important because no matter how much research we do considering teachers' views or even leaders' views in schools, there is never a greater measure of importance than how students feel and perceive their learning experience. These studies are categorized by the subject area in which the study took place.

Science and CRE

To better understand the impact of social justice science education, Dimick (2012) studied one White male environmental science teacher, Mr. Carson, whose urban high school class consisted of 24 Black students. Carson implemented a culturally responsive social justice project in his classroom, titled The Green River Project, to give students an experiential learning opportunity to study one of the most polluted rivers in the country and how "environmental pollutants disproportionately affect people of color and poor communities" (Dimick, 2012, p. 999). This science project took students outside of the classroom to see how social injustices, related to the science content, were applicable in their own environment and to research possible ways to combat such injustices.

Dimick (2012) acting as a participant-observer in the classroom over one semester, reviewed the curriculum and texts used in class, conducted multiple interviews with the environmental science teacher, and facilitated five focus groups with nine students who represented the low to high range of academic ability found in the class. The focus group students reported the educational experiences in the environmental science class allowed them to link the things they learned in class to actual events occurring in their community and raise their "consciousness about the environmental problems and, by extension, social injustices they experienced living near the river" (p. 999). Dimick (2012) concluded that the nine Black students became more engaged in the science class and attained a sense of empowerment due to the class' projects that connected them to the community.

Basu and Barton (2010) came to similar conclusions when studying 21 students of color and their ideas about teachers using Democratic Science Pedagogy, which provided an opportunity to engage in a "less authoritarian, more democratic relationship between teachers and students in which students have increased choice, voice, and authority" (p. 74). One example reported by a student included having options to read a science text that related to their own interests. The researchers noted this increased engagement as key to unlocking the potential of students of color in the classroom.

While engagement and empowerment matters, the following research studies explored academic achievement in culturally responsive science classrooms. For example, Laughter and Adams (2012) employed the use of qualitative methods to study the outcome of culturally relevant science teaching in an urban characteristic middle school science classroom. The term *urban characteristic* refers to a school that faces similar challenges as an urban school, although it is not necessarily located in a major city. Through semi-structured interviews, observations, and classroom artifacts (i.e., student-generated discussion lab questions related to the reading), Laughter and Adams studied one teacher's implementation of a culturally relevant science unit and its impact on the students.

Laughter and Adams (2012) found that students were more eager to grapple with the science curriculum and engage with the academic language in a meaningful way when the information was couched in their personal worldview. Students began to understand science as a means to combat social injustices around them. Laughter and Adams concluded that culturally responsive science is essential for advancing the equality in science agenda to which many educators claim to subscribe. Students relating to the content and viewing it as a vehicle to improve the communities they occupy is the true mark of academic achievement.

Similarly, Boutte et al. (2010) studied the instructional practices of a teacher implementing culturally relevant science instruction with Black students in a high school classroom in an effort to "bridge the distances between school instruction and ways of knowing and realities within the homes and communities of culturally diverse students" (p. 2). One example of a culturally responsive lesson required students to draw comparisons between cell structures and items they encounter in everyday life. Instead of giving all students the same teacher-generated terms to memorize, this lesson allowed students to make original analogies based on things that were memorable to them. After creating the analogies, the students created collages using visuals that related the science concepts to their everyday experiences.

The teacher in this case study also exposed students to Black scientists who may not have been included in the curriculum to enable them to understand and identify with the broader contributions of non-White scientists. This intentional exposure to diverse scientists allowed the students to see scholars who looked like them. Through the analysis of several culturally responsive classroom science activities, Boutte et al. (2010) discovered that when the teacher implemented the culturally relevant science instruction students had higher passing grades on vocabulary tests and gained the ability to use the academic vocabulary and concepts, they acquired in science class in their everyday lives (e.g., considering which hair/skin products to purchase, understanding product safety testing procedures).

In the same vein, Stevens, Andrade, and Page (2016) studied a culturally relevant science program for Native American elementary and secondary students. This program made a point to construct science learning to draw on students' prior knowledge and linked them to new concepts. For instance, when learning about the earth, space, and soil, students were given opportunities to leave the classroom and textbooks behind and venture to a local agriculture center to study the practices of Native Americans' and desert farming (Stevens et al., 2016). This unit also included lessons on how to create edible soil, Native American soil paintings, and careers related to soil science in general. According to the researchers, these practices "led [students] to greater understanding... and the ability to re-teach others, thereby increasing their self-efficacy and their pride in their culture" (Stevens et al., 2016, p. 958). Intentional connections to the culture and heritage of this historically marginalized student group motivated them to engage in the content, which resulted in improved academic achievement (Stevens et al., 2016).

These studies highlight some of the success seen with CRE in science classrooms, specifically. The research suggests that culturally responsive approaches to instruction left students of color more engaged, motivated, empowered, and/or achieving academically. The following section explores the research available on Math and CRE, another subject presumed to be context-neutral by many.

Math and CRE

Even though there is limited research available on CRE and science, more studies at all school levels were focused on CRE and math. Hubert (2013) conducted a case study in a high school mathematics class where the teacher employed CRE practices. Specifically, while the 37 students in the class were studying quadratic and exponential functions, the students were given opportunities to select lessons that covered a range of topics that were responsive to their interests and rooted in real-life scenarios. These topics included teen pregnancy, HIV, teen smoking, football, soccer, and saving money.

Hubert (2013) interviewed five of the students (i.e., two Black, one mixed race, one White, and one Hispanic student) 2 weeks after the conclusion of the 10-day CRE intervention to explore their perceptions of using culturally relevant pedagogy (CRP) in the class. He found the students appreciated having options to choose lessons based on their interests. For example, one student reported feeling she "could relate to the teen pregnancy lessons because her sister is a teenager and has two babies" (p. 330).

In all, Hubert's (2013) five participants reported improved attitudes and greater interest in mathematics because of the CRP-driven content. Creating these organic connections to the students' lives increased their willingness to engage with the content of the math class and motivated students intrinsically (Hubert, 2013).

Fulton (2009) similarly discovered that middle school students reported having a deeper understanding of the math content as a result of their teachers' commitment to using culturally responsive teaching. In this qualitative case study, Fulton (2009) conducted classroom observations where she discovered teachers using specific practices (i.e., individual, small, and whole group problem solving; incorporating thinking strategies; and using problems that covered important content and were engaging) in an effort to create more culturally responsive classrooms.

In addition to teacher interviews, Fulton (2009) conducted focus groups with 12 participating students to get an understanding of their perspectives on the effectiveness of the practices their teachers used in the classroom. In the focus groups, students reported feeling a deeper connection to the math content in addition to gaining a better understanding of each other's perspectives. Fulton (2009) concluded, "through constant and deliberate uses of specific [culturally responsive] teaching behaviors... teachers in my study were able to produce learning environments that allowed students who have expanded ideas about mathematics and healthy notions about their own ability to be successful as mathematical thinkers" (p. 107). This sense of empowerment described by the students in this study is quintessential for more students of color to experience academic achievement.

Likewise, Cholewa, Goodman, West-Olatunji, and Amatea (2014) found that, as early as elementary school, culturally responsive practices positively impacted students of color in math. In their study of an outstanding 5th-grade math teacher, Ms. Morris, who was nominated by parents and the principal as an effective teacher at a school with majority Black students, they concluded her success was rooted in her commitment to "building on experiences and existing knowledge, integrating music and dance, and utilizing familiar communications styles" (Cholewa et al., 2014, p. 581). The researchers noted that students in Ms. Morris' classes exhibited positive characteristics that included "zest, empowerment, clarity, sense of worth, and feelings of connection" (Cholewa et al., 2014, p. 579). This study further illustrated that CRE practices have the power to motivate and empower students of various ages when they are properly implemented.

The previous studies were focused on small case studies, but Langlie (2008) used the 1988 National Educational Longitudinal Study database to explore how Black and Hispanic 10th-grade students were impacted by their math teachers' use of culturally responsive practices. To determine the relationship between CRP practices and student achievement, Langlie conducted standard multiple regression analysis and concluded that teachers who emphasized math in the everyday lives of the students "encourage their students to become interested in mathematics and encourage students to understand the applications of mathematics... achieve more in mathematics" (p. 6). Cultural responsiveness takes foreign content and connects it directly to the knowledge that students of color possess. This kind of connection is a major tenet of CRE and is a hallmark of academic achievement.

The next two sections include literature on English/language arts and social studies, as they shed light on students' perceptions of their learning motivation and empowerment and the impact of CRE in the classroom. These studies illustrate that when teachers make concerted efforts to use culturally relevant instruction in their classrooms, students not only feel more connected to the content, but they also feel empowered to succeed.

English/Language Arts and CRE

Implementation of CRE has been linked to increased student motivation in ELA classrooms. Hill (2012) used a mixed-methods approach to study two teachers' culturally responsive practices and their perceptions of those practices with 24 high school students on the South Side of Chicago. Through the teachers' use of specific methods, such as cultural metaphors and personally relevant examples, discussion circles, and teaching literacy skills from basic to complex, students reported feeling motivated in the English class. Further, they gained a sense of connectedness to the curriculum and how it applied to their personal lives (Hill, 2012).

Christianakis (2011) reached similar results in a study that looked at the impact of a language arts teachers' use of rap music in a 5th-grade classroom. Using rap and poetry in conjunction with the language arts curriculum made students report feeling more engaged and motivated to do the work required of them.

In another study with elementary-aged students in a language arts classroom, Bui and Fagen (2013) explored if the teachers' use of culturally responsive teaching approaches (i.e., story grammar instruction, word webs, activating prior knowledge, prediction strategies, multicultural literature and cooperative learning) led to increases in student learning. Bui and Fagen reported one group of students moved from frustration level to being ready for instruction according to the data from the pretest and posttest provided by the 49 participants. While no one instructional practice claimed to fix all of the educational disparities with these students of color, the utilization of CRT practices helped them move past their initial frustrations with the content and connected them with the learning in the classroom.

Duncan-Andrade (2007) studied four highly effective English teachers in elementary and high school, over 3 years, in southern Los Angeles. The teachers were selected to participate because they were recommended by their peers and campus leaders, their students attained good grades and test scores, and they utilized social justice pedagogy for equalizing the voices of marginalized cultures with the voices of the dominant culture. For example, instead of using the scripted curriculum's persuasive writing prompt asking students to write about choosing teams at recess, one of the teachers in the study created a prompt requiring students to write a persuasive letter to their principal discussing a problem they experienced in the school and why it was important to fix it. The project culminated with students writing letters to their superintendent, and one student-selected representative sharing his letter and voicing legitimate concerns for change in their schools and community.

In the end, Duncan-Andrade (2007) discovered five common practices that emerged as pillars for success with the participating teachers in urban school settings. First, *critically conscious purpose* referred to the teachers' ability to build "intellectually rigorous lessons that are relevant to the real and immediate conditions of their students' lives so that students can think and respond critically for themselves" (Duncan-Andrade, 2007, p. 627). Second, *duty* represented the teachers' sense of responsibility and connectedness to the communities in which they taught. Third, *preparation* meant these teachers spent time preparing for classes, as they gathered resources to supplement scripted curriculum. Fourth, *Socratic sensibility* described the teachers' ability to exhibit great "balance between confidence in their ability as teachers and frequent self-critique" (Duncan-Andrade, 2007, p. 632). Fifth, *trust* referred to the teachers' willingness to proceed with the notion that reliance must be established and maintained with students in urban populations, as students do not automatically bestow trust on educators.

Duncan-Andrade (2007) found that the participating teachers' commitment to implementing these five pillars of effective practice in urban settings led to their students' academic successes. Although the curriculum may vary from science and math to language arts, this body of research suggests the same types of engagement, empowerment, and academic achievement can be possible when aspects of CRE are implemented with fidelity in the classroom.

Social Studies and CRE

Considered by many to be one of the more ideal subject matters for cultural responsiveness and cultivating social justice, social studies research also reported great benefits for student outcomes in classrooms. For example, Martell (2013), a White male, examined his own New York high school history class in which he incorporated culturally relevant teaching in several ways. For example, he included reading materials related to the backgrounds of his students, used diverse accounts of history that included people of color, and required students to write research papers where they reflected on their cultures in relation to American history.

In the study, Martell (2013) conducted interviews with three Hispanic students and one Black student regarding their perceptions of CRT practices in the class. In the end, he found the interview participants felt empowered by the way he used these culturally relevant practices to connect their racial backgrounds to the content taught in history class. Second, Martell administered a survey to all his students ($n = 74$) and compared responses by race between Black and White students with independent sample t-tests and found that both Black and White students responded similarly to the items, regardless of race. The survey data revealed 71.4% of the Black and Hispanic students liked learning about history as a result of the CRT pedagogy used, and 81.7% of the Black and Hispanic students reported recalling more historical information from this class compared to their recollection of what they learned in previous history classes.

Coughran (2012) also explored the impact of culturally relevant pedagogy in her elementary school social science classroom by incorporating students' lived experiences of race in society with her curriculum. Based on post-lesson discussions and student interviews, students reported feeling more connected to the curriculum and to each other. The ability to make standard curriculum more dynamic for diverse groups of students is evident in the responses of the students who reported feeling excited about learning the content and engaging in the classroom activities.

Even though Martell (2013) and Coughran (2012) reported positive findings about the use of CRP in the classroom, their findings might be considered suspect because they used their own classrooms for their studies (Gall, Gall, & Borg, 2003). On the other hand, Choi (2013) researched the effectiveness of an exemplary (as identified through snowball sampling and community nominations) social studies teacher, Mr. Moon, and his implementation of CRP at a public high school that served students from more than 50 countries. Choi gathered data for this case study through classroom observations, three 1-hour interviews with Mr. Moon, and artifacts (i.e., handouts, quizzes, and homework) over 6 months.

Choi (2013) reported that Mr. Moon challenged the standard curriculum by including the history and experiences of the students he served. For instance, he designed a "month-long unit on China addressing the dynamic geographical characteristics of China... and he led group projects in topographical map making" (Choi, 2013, p. 14). Choi found that students' academic engagement and achievement increased "as evidenced and observed by their active participation in learning, critical thinking/analysis skills development, and cooperative knowledge construction" (p. 17). Choi credited the implementation of CRP in Moon's social studies class for the positive outcomes.

Durm (2016) conducted a study specifically of the experiences of Black male students in social studies classes at different schools. The teachers noted their intentionality in combating stereotypes by discussing historical figures who were otherwise not included in the school's traditional texts. The students reported feeling positive about their social studies teachers, as well as empowered by learning about their own history. The students also acknowledged that when they learned about the resilience demonstrated by their ancestors in history, the exposure moved them from feelings of victimhood to agents of change (Durm, 2016). This is the power of cultural responsiveness in the social studies classroom.

In the end, the CRE researchers reported that culturally responsive practices helped increase students' motivation, engagement, empowerment, and academic performance. Also, the CRE researchers noted that gaining cultural awareness caused teachers to learn about their students so that students and teachers could become partners in the pursuit of social justice.

Conclusion

You can do this! You can be a FRESH teacher! Whether you're a brand-spanking-new teacher or an OG, if you have read to this point in the book, you already have one thing that is necessary on the journey, a heart to do something FRESH. You want to connect with your students in ways that are authentic and transformational. You don't want to just play school and maintain the status quo. You understand the role that schools play in the struggle for social justice and creating a more just world for ALL God's children, and you don't take your part in that equation lightly. Congratulations to you on committing to not only keeping your classroom FRESH, sometimes, but pledging to become more consistent with these best practices at all times.

Implementing the strategies, you've learned here will not always be easy. There will be obstacles to execution. Trust me. As a principal, I drove my fair share of vans and little buses to ensure transportation for a group of scholars. As the girl's mentorship group sponsor, I booked hotel rooms during our college tour, only to arrive at the hotel and be told that it was an adults-only hotel (clearly, I neglected to read the fine print). As an ELAR teacher hosting my "Poetry Café" to showcase students' work after the poetry unit, someone broke into my classroom and stole all the Starbucks drinks, food, and pastries I purchased for my students (with my own money) the evening before the event. The point I'm trying to make is that the work is hard, but even so, it's worth it. So, start by focusing on a couple of things and add more as you go!

To this day, I still hear from students and their parents who rave about the different experiences they had and remember all these years later and what those experiences meant to them. None of them ever say how thankful they are that I prepared them to ace the state assessment (even if I know that was one of the instructional goals for the year). They always recall the Great Debates on Fridays, or trips to this or that college, or some presentation they did and how proud they were of their work. Those students are my "Mona Lisa." They taught me how to dig deep and connect. That is the legacy I am working to achieve daily.

What will your legacy be? A teacher who maintained the status quo and did what was required to get a good evaluation from year to year while counting down the days to the next break? Or will you be a FRESH Classroom Teacher who serves as a game-changer for students? The choice is yours to make. Not just today, but every contract day you show up in your classroom. Make every day a FRESH day because culturally relevant education just can't wait, and neither can your students!

References and Resources

ACT. (2016a). *The Condition of College & Career Readiness 2016.* https://www.act.org/content/dam/act/unsecured/documents/CCCR_National_2016.pdf

ACT. (2016b). *The Condition of STEM 2016.* http://www.act.org/content/dam/act/unsecured/documents/STEM2016_52_National.pdf

Al-Fadhli, H. M., & Kersen, T. M. (2010). How religious, social, and cultural capital factors influence educational aspirations of African American Adolescents. *Journal of Negro Education, 79*(3), 380-389. https://www.jstor.org/stable/20798356

Aronson, B., & Laughter, J. (2016). The theory and practice of culturally relevant education: A synthesis of research across content areas. *Review of Educational Research, 86*(1), 163-206. doi:10.3102/0034654315582066

Basu, S. J., & Barton, A. C. (2010). A researcher-student-teacher model for democratic science pedagogy: Connections to community, shared authority, and critical science agency. *Equity & Excellence in Education, 43*(1), 72-87. doi:10.1080/10665680903489379

Beede, D., Julian, T., Khan, B., Lehrman, R., McKittrick, G., Langdon, D., & Doms, M. (2011). *Education supports racial and ethnic equality in STEM (ESA Issue Brief No. 05-11).* http://www.esa.doc.gov/sites/default/files/education_supports_racial_and_ethnic_equality_in_stem.pdf

Bonner, E. P. & Adams, T. L. (2011). Culturally responsive teaching in the context of mathematics: a grounded theory case study. *Journal of Math Teacher Education, 15,* 25-38.

Boutte, G., Kelly-Jackson, C., & Johnson, G. (2010). Culturally relevant teaching in science classrooms: addressing academic achievement, cultural competence, and critical consciousness. *International Journal of Multicultural Education, 12*(2), 1-20. http://ijme-journal.org/index.php/ijme/article/viewFile/343/512

Brown, J. C., & Crippen, K. J. (2016). The growing awareness inventory: Building capacity for culturally responsive science and mathematics with a structured observation protocol. School Science and Mathematics, 116(3), 127-138. doi:10.1111/ssm.12163

Bui, Y. N., & Fagan, Y. M. (2013). The effects of an integrated reading comprehension strategy: A culturally responsive teaching approach for fifth-grade students' reading comprehension. Preventing School Failure, 57(2), 59-69. doi:10.1080/1045988X.2012.664581

Choi, Y. (2013). Teaching social studies for newcomer English language learners: Toward culturally relevant pedagogy. Multicultural Perspectives, 15(1), 12-18. doi:10.1080/15210960.2013.754640

Cholewa, B., Goodman, R. D., West-Olatunji, C., & Amatea, E. (2014). A qualitative examination of the impact of culturally responsive educational practices on the psychological well-being of students of color. The Urban Review, 46(4), 574-596. doi:10.1007/s11256-014-0272

Christianakis, M. (2011). Hybrid texts: Fifth graders, rap music, and writing. Urban Education, 46(5), 1131-1168. doi:10.1177/0042085911400326

Colbert, P. J. (2010). Developing a culturally responsive classroom collaborative of faculty, students, and institution. Contemporary Issues in Education Research, 3(9), 17-26.

Coughran, M. J. (2012). Enacting Culturally Relevant Pedagogy: Going Beyond Heroes and Holidays Curriculum (Doctoral dissertation). ProQuest Dissertations & Theses Global database. (UMI No. 1510828)

Dimick, A. S. (2012). Student empowerment in an environmental science classroom: Toward a framework for social justice science education. Science Education, 96(6), 990-1012. doi:10.1002/sce.21035

Duncan-Andrade, J. (2007). Gangstas, wankstas, and ridas: Defining, developing, and supporting effective teachers in urban schools. International Journal of Qualitative Studies in Education, 20(6), 617-638. doi:10.1080/09518390701630767

Durm, T. C. (2016). Focus on teacher education: Social studies and the Black male: Culturally responsive curricula. Childhood Education, 92(6), 497-499. doi:10.1080/00094056.2016.1251800

Ellis, J. B., Abreu-Ellis, C., Moore, A., Aukerman, K., Buttil, M., & Edwards, A. (2017). Developing cultural responsiveness while teaching content standards: Lessons from a Brazilian experience. *American Secondary Education, 45*(2), 69-84.

Emdin, C. (2016). *For White Folks Who Teach in the Hood – and the Rest of Y'all Too: Reality Pedagogy and Urban Education.* Beacon Press.

Esposito, J., & Swain, A. N. (2009). Pathways to social justice: Urban teachers' uses of culturally relevant pedagogy as a conduit for teaching for social justice. *Perspectives on urban education, 6*(Spring), 38-48. http://files.eric.ed.gov/fulltext/EJ838745.pdf

Fulton, R. (2009). *A Case Study of Culturally Responsive Teaching in Middle School Mathematics* (Doctoral dissertation). ProQuest Dissertations & Theses Global database. (UMI No. 3372472)

Gall, M. D., Gall, J. P., & Borg, W. R. (2003). *Educational Research: An Introduction* (7th ed.). Pearson.

Gay, G. (2002). Preparing for culturally responsive teaching. *Journal of Teacher Education, 53*(1), 106-116. doi:10.1177%2F0022487102053002003

Gay, G. (2010). *Culturally Responsive Teaching: Theory, Research, and Practice* (2nd ed.). Teachers College Press.

Gay, G. (2013). Teaching to and through cultural diversity. *Curriculum Inquiry, 43*(1), 48-70. doi:10.1111/curi.12002

Goodlad, J., Mantle-Bromley, C., & Goodlad, S. J. (2004). *Education for everyone: Agenda for education in a democracy.* San Francisco, CA: Jossey-Bass.

Hernandez, C. M., Morales, A. R., & Shroyer, M. G. (2013). The development of a model of culturally responsive science and mathematics teaching. *Cultural Studies of Science Education, 8*(4), 803-820. doi:10.1007/s11422-013-9544-1

Hill, A. L. (2012). *Culturally responsive teaching: An investigation of effective practices for African American learners* (Doctoral dissertation). ProQuest Dissertations & Theses Global database. (UMI No. 3549438)

Hubert, T. L. (2013). Learners of mathematics: High school students' perspectives of culturally relevant mathematics pedagogy. *Journal of African American Studies, 18*(3), 324-336. doi:10.1007/s12111-013-9273-2

Irvine, J. J. (2010). Foreword. In H. R. Milner's (Ed.), Culture, curriculum, and identity in education (pp. xi-xvi). Palgrave Macmillan.

Johnson, C. C. (2011). The road to culturally relevant science: Exploring how teachers navigate change in pedagogy. Journal of Research in Science Teaching, 48(2), 170-198. doi:10.1002/tea.20405

Ladson-Billings, G. (1994). The dreamkeepers: Successful teachers of African American children. San Francisco, CA: Jossey-Bass.

Ladson-Billings, G. (1995a). But that's just good teaching! The case for culturally relevant pedagogy. Theory into Practice, 43(3), 159-165. doi:10.1080/00405849509543675

Ladson-Billings, G. (1995b). Toward a theory of culturally relevant pedagogy. American Educational Research Journal, 32(3), 465-491. http://links.jstor.org/sici?sici=0002-8312%2819952%2932%3A3%3C465%3ATATOCR%3E2.0.CO%3B2-4

Ladson-Billings, G. (2006). "Yes, but how do we do it?" Practicing culturally relevant pedagogy. In J. G. Landsman & C. W. Lewis (Eds.), White teachers' diverse classrooms: Creating inclusive schools, building on students' diversity, and providing true educational equity (pp. 33-46). Sterling, VA: Stylus.

Ladson-Billings, G. (2014). Culturally relevant pedagogy 2.0: a.k.a. the remix. Harvard Educational Review, 84(1), 74-84. doi:10.17763/haer.84.1.p2rj131485484751

Landivar, L. C. (2013). Disparities in STEM Employment by sex, race, and Hispanic origin: American community survey reports. Washington, DC: U.S. Department of Commerce, U.S. Census Bureau. https://www.census.gov/prod/2013pubs/acs-24.pdf

Langlie, M. L. (2008). The effect of culturally relevant pedagogy on the mathematics achievement of Black and Hispanic high school students (Doctoral dissertation). Proquest Dissertations and Theses Database. (UMI No. 3304098)

Lindsey, D. B., Jungwirth, L. D., Pahl, J. V. N. C., & Lindsey, R. B. (2009). Culturally proficient learning communities: Confronting inequities through collaborative curiosity. Corwin.

Lortie, D. (2002). Schoolteacher: A sociological study (2nd ed.). University of Chicago

Press.

Martell, C. C. (2013). Race and histories: Examining culturally relevant teaching in the U.S. history classroom. Theory & Research in Social Education, 41(1), 65-88. doi:10.1080/00933104.2013.755745

Mayer, M., & Phillips, V. L. (2012). Primary sources: 2012 America's teachers on the teaching profession. Scholastic, Bill & Melinda Gates Foundation. http://www.scholastic.com/primarysources/

Mensah, F. M. (2011). A case for culturally relevant teaching in science education and lessons learned for teacher education. The Journal of Negro Education, 80(3), 296-309.

Milner, H. R., IV. (2011). Culturally relevant pedagogy in a diverse urban classroom. The Urban Review, 43(1), 66-89. doi:10.1007/s11256-009-0143-0

Milner, H. R., IV. (2012). Beyond a test score: Explaining opportunity gaps in educational practice. Journal of Black Studies, 43(6), 693-718. doi:10.1177/0021934712442539

National Center for Education Statistics. (2015). Digest of education statistics: Table 318.45, number and percentage distribution of science, technology, engineering, and mathematics (STEM) degrees/certificates conferred by postsecondary institutions, by race/ethnicity, level of degree/certificate, and sex of student: 2008-09 through 2012-13. Washington, DC: U.S. Department of Education. https://nces.ed.gov/programs/digest/d14/tables/dt14_318.45.asp

National Science and Technology Council. (2013, June). Federal science, technology, engineering, and mathematics (STEM) education 5-year strategic plan: A report from the committee on STEM education. https://www.aip.org/fyi/2013/national-science-and-technology-councils-committee-stem-education-releases-5-year-strategic

Ndunda, M., Sickle, M. V., Perry, L., & Capelloni, A. (2017). University-urban high school partnership: Math and science professional learning communities. School Science and Mathematics, 117(3-4), 137-145. doi:10.1111/ssm.12215

Reeves, P. M., Hung, W. P., & Sun, C. K. (2017). Influence of teacher collaboration on job satisfaction and student achievement. Teaching and Teacher Education, 67, 227-236. doi:10.1016/j.tate.2017.06.016

Rinke, C. R. (2009). Exploring the generation gap in urban schools: Generational perspectives in professional learning communities. Education and Urban Society, 42(1), 3-24. doi:10.1177/0013124509342699

Ronfeldt, M., Farmer, S. O., McQueen, K., & Grissom, J. A. (2015). Teacher collaboration in instructional teams and student achievement. American Educational Research Journal, 52(3) 475-514. doi:10.3102/0002831215585562

Rychly, L., & Graves, E. (2012). Teacher characteristics for culturally responsive pedagogy. Multicultural Perspectives, 14, 44-49. doi:10.1080/15210960.2012.646853

Saifer, S., Edwards, K., Ellis, D., Ko, L., & Stuczynski, A. (2011). Culturally responsive standards-based teaching. Corwin.

Saltman, K. (2014). The politics of education: A critical introduction. Boulder, CO: Paradigm.

Snively, G., & Corsiglia, J. (2001). Discovering indigenous science: Implications for science education. Science Education, 85(1), 6-34. doi:10.1002/1098-237X(200101)85:1<6::AID-SCE3>3.0.CO;2-R

Stevens, S., Andrade, R., & Page, M. (2016). Motivating young native American students to pursue STEM learning through a culturally relevant science program. Journal of Science Education and Technology, 25(6), 947-960. doi:10.1007/s10956-016-9629-1

U.S. Census Bureau. (2016). Quick facts. https://www.census.gov/quickfacts/

Vescio, V., Ross, D., & Adams, A. (2008). A review of research on the impact of professional learning communities on teaching practice and student learning. Teaching and Teacher Education, 24(1), 80-91. doi:10.1016/j.tate.2007.01.004

Vilorio, D. (2014). STEM 101: Intro to tomorrow's jobs. http://www.bls.gov/careeroutlook/2014/spring/art01.pdf

Woodland, R. H. (2016). Evaluating pk-12 professional learning communities: An improvement science perspective. American Journal of Evaluation, 37(4), 505-521. doi:10.1177/1098214016634203

Yosso, T. (2005). Whose culture has capital? A critical race theory discussion of community cultural wealth. Race Ethnicity and Education, 8(1), 69-91. https://doi.org/10.1080/1361332052000341006

Acknowledgments

All praises to God, the father, for entrusting me with the gift and guiding me on the journey. I am nothing without your grace that has proved to be sufficient in every season.

To the ancestors who fought for rights and privileges I am blessed to take for granted. I am humbled and proud to have your blood coursing through my veins. I am because you are.

To my loving husband Chris. Who knew this journey would bring us here? I'm blessed to do life with you every day, and there isn't another person I'd rather do it with. You are my rock. Thanks for always holding me down.

To my mommy. You've always been a pillar of strength and showed me what faith in God looks like in action. I am a Proverbs 31 woman because I first saw one in real life.

To my dad. Words can't explain how much our relationship means to me. I see your grind and I've learned that hard things are possible, if I set my mind and intentions on them. I'm built like a thoroughbred because of you.

To my family, friends, and colleagues that have prayed for me, encouraged me to keep writing, shared information, watched my kid, spoke life to me, etc. It takes a village, and I'm grateful that you are mine.

About the Author

Dr. Stephanie R. Boyce is an edupreneur driven by her passion to reshape the educational landscape by making FRESH Classrooms an everyday phenomenon. For more than a decade, Boyce has focused her studies and work on matters of racial justice and equity for historically marginalized groups with a focus on educational spaces. She currently serves as the Chief Education Officer of Stephanie Boyce & Associates, LLC., Director of The FRESH Classroom (a non-profit organization), Professor & Director of the Writing Program at Paul Quinn College, and Lecturer of African American Studies at the University of Houston.

For more information about Dr. Boyce and booking details visit www.stephanieboyce.com or email us at info@stephanieboyce.com.

Follow Dr. Boyce on IG and Twitter @DrSRBoyce.

For more information about The FRESH Classroom (a non-profit organization) visit www.thefreshclassroom.com.

Follow The FRESH Classroom on Facebook and IG @FreshClassroom and Twitter @Fresh_Classroom.

Made in United States
North Haven, CT
07 November 2021